In My Indian Garden

Philip Stewart Robinson

In the interest of creating a more extensive selection of rare historical book reprints, we have chosen to reproduce this title even though it may possibly have occasional imperfections such as missing and blurred pages, missing text, poor pictures, markings, dark backgrounds and other reproduction issues beyond our control. Because this work is culturally important, we have made it available as a part of our commitment to protecting, preserving and promoting the world's literature. Thank you for your understanding.

IN MY INDIAN GARDEN.

BY

PHIL. ROBINSON.

WITH A PREFACE BY

EDWIN ARNOLD, M.A., C.S.I., F.R.G.S., &c., &c.

THIRD EDITION.

London:
SAMPSON LOW, MARSTON, SEARLE, & RIVINGTON,
CROWN BUILDINGS, 188, FLEET STREET.
1878.
[All rights reserved.]

INSCRIBED

TO

SIR H. DRUMMOND WOLFF, M.P.,

IN MEMORY OF PAST KINDNESS,

BY THE AUTHOR.

PREFACE.

I HAVE derived so much pleasure from reading the following sketches, humorous and pathetic, of Indian incidents, scenes, and objects, that I am glad to have the opportunity of recommending them to the two classes of readers who will, I think, be chiefly interested. One class consists of those who desire to know—what is not at present to be found in books—the out-of-door ordinary themes of observation in India; the other class, of those who—knowing India well, and all the familiar sights and sounds alluded to in this little volume—will easily fill up the slight and pleasant outline of the Author's sketches, and thus renew for themselves many and many a bygone happy hour and old association of their Eastern home. None but Anglo-Indians know what a treasure-mine of art, literature, and picturesque description lies unworked in the common experiences of our life in India. But some are unobservant; some are too soon familiarized and forget the charm of first impressions; some admire, or are amused, but lack the gift of expression; and nearly all official Indians have too much business to leave them time for the pursuit or record of natural history, and such light and laughing science as this little book contains. For here I think is one bright exception: one Anglo-Indian who has not only felt the never-ceasing attraction of the "common objects" of India for a cultivated and observant fancy, but has found time and gifts to record them as they first struck him, in a style which, with all its lightness of manner and material, has great strength and value, like those fine webs of Dacca and Delhi with the embroidered beetle-wings and feathers. The Author writes of beetles, birds, frogs, squirrels, and the "small deer" of India, but always, as it seems to me, with so just a sense of the vivid vitality of these Indian scenes and creatures, and so much sympathy for the Asiatic side of our empire, down to its simplest every-day objects, that I should not know where to send an uninformed English reader for better hints of the out-of-door look and spirit of things in our Indian gardens.

Preface.

They are only sketches, no doubt, which fill this little portfolio, but their outlines are often drawn with so true a hand, that nothing can be more suggestive to the memory of any one who has lived the same life. India may be hot, dusty, distant, and whatever else the weary exile alleges when his liver goes wrong, but she is never for one moment, or in any spot, as regards her people, her scenery, her cities, towns, villages, or country-places, vulgar. There is nothing in her not worth study and regard; for the stamp of a vast past is over all the land, and the very pariah-dogs are classic to those who know Indian fables and how to be entertained by them. Our Author is one of the happy few in whom familiarity with Indian sights and objects has not bred indifference, but rather suggested the beginnings of a new field of Anglo-Indian literature. If I am not wrong, the charm of looking at these utterly common-place animals and people of India in this gay and pleased spirit is, that we get that freshness of feeling, which youth alone enjoys when all the world is new to it, interpreted by the adult and matured mind, suddenly entering a practically new world, for such India is to the English official on his first arrival. All we other Indians had of course noticed all those odd and tender points about the "syce's children," the "pea-boy," the "bheesty's mother," the "dâk-bungalow moorghees," the "mynas," crows, green parrots, squirrels, and the beetles that get into the mustard and the soup. Here, however, is one at last who writes down his observations, and opens, I think, thereby a rich and charming field of Indian literature, which ought hereafter to yield many other pages as agreeable as those which it gives me true satisfaction thus to commend to the public.

EDWIN ARNOLD.

PREFATORY INDEX.

Part I.

IN MY INDIAN GARDEN.

"When God set about creation, He first planted a garden."
Nugæ Orielanæ.

                                            PAGE

THE BIRDS 1

"*Euel.*—But of what sort, pray, is this life among the birds? for you know it accurately.
Hoopoe.—Not an unpleasant one to pass; where, in the first place, we must live without a purse.
Euel.—You have removed much of life's base metal.
Hoopoe.—And we feed in gardens upon the white sesame and myrtle-berries and poppies and mint."
Aristophanes (Hickie's).

OF HENS 7

"Tame, villatic fowl."—*Milton.*
"The feathered tribe domestic."—*Cowper.*
"The careful hen."—*Thomson.*
"The dâk-bungalow fowls develope the bones of vultures and lay the eggs of finches."—*Nugæ Orielanæ.*

Prefatory Index.

	PAGE
CORVUS SPLENDENS	15

"'Crows,' remarked the Ettrick Shepherd, 'are down in the devil's book in round-hand.'"—*Noctes Ambrosianæ.*

GREEN PARROTS 20

"The writer of the Mahabharata excluded green parrots from an ideal country. 'There are,' he writes, 'no parrots there to eat the grain.'"—*Nugæ Orielanæ.*

THE MYNAS (*Sturninæ*) 24

"To strange mysterious dulness still the friends.—*Byron.*
"Two starlings cannot sleep in one bed."—*Proverb.*

THE SEVEN SISTERS 30

"One for each of the wise men of Greece, one for each hill of Rome, each of the *divitis ostia Nili* and each hero of Thebes, one for each day of the week, one for each of the Pleiades, one for each cardinal sin."—*Nugæ Orielanæ.*

THE MUNGOOSE 33

THE GREY SQUIRREL 36

"The squirrel Adjidauno,
In and out among the branches,
Cough'd and chatter'd in the oak-tree,
Laugh'd and said between his laughing,
Do not shoot me, Hiawatha."
Longfellow.

THE ANTS 39

"To the emmet gives
Her foresight and the intelligence that makes
The tiny creatures strong by social league."
Wordsworth.

"The parsimonious emmet."—*Milton.*
"Us vagrant emmets."—*Young.*

Prefatory Index.

THE PARIAH DOG AND THE CAT 45

"As all criminals are countrymen, so all pariah dogs are brothers."—*Nugæ Orielanæ.*

"That the old Egyptians should have venerated the dog I can understand, but to hold THE CAT sacred! If the priests of Nepthys want a few cat-mummies I will furnish their temples handsomely for them."—*Ibid.*

THE PEA-BOY 47

"A thing of dark imaginings."—*Lara.*

THE FRUITS 49

"Fruit of all kinds, in coat
Rough or smooth, rind, a bearded husk, or shell."
Paradise Lost.

THE FROGS 51

"'The croaking of frogs,' said Luther, 'edifies nothing at all. It is mere sophistry and fruitless.'"—*Colloquia Mensalia.*

Part II.

THE INDIAN SEASONS.

SUB JOVE FERVIDO 59

"A great length of deadly days."
Atalanta in Calydon.

SUB JOVE PLUVIO 73

> "Forth fly the tepid airs and unconfined,
> Unbinding earth, the moving softness strays;
> Joyous, the impatient husbandman perceives
> Relenting nature, and his lusty steers
> Drives from the stalls to where the well-used plough
>   Lies in the furrow."—*Thomson's Seasons.*

SUB JOVE BENIGNO 96

Part III.

AMONG THE CROPS.

AMONG THE CROPS 113

> "And the grace of standing corn."—*Morris.*

THE SPARROW 116

> "'The sparrow,' said Luther, 'is a most voracious animal, and does great harm to the crops. The Hebrews call it "tschirp," and it should be killed wherever found.'"—*Colloquia Mensalia.*

THE WOLF 119

> "Of the heraldic bearings of the tribes of Israel nearly all are commonplace and plainly '*aperte*' in their significations. Thus, the ox of Joseph and of Ephraim, the young lion of Judah and the eagle of Dan. But two are peculiarly suggestive, the triple wave on the shield of Reuben, 'unstable as water,' and Benjamin's wolf couched in the field of green corn."—*Nugæ Orielanæ.*

Prefatory Index.

	PAGE
THE JACKALS	122

"Scenes form'd for contemplation and to nurse
The growing seeds of wisdom, ...
Scenes such as these 'tis his supreme delight
To fill with riot."—*The Task.*

SUDHOO	126

BUGGOO, THE CHOWKEYDAR	130

"His life is a watch or a vision,
Between a sleep and a sleep."
Atalanta in Calydon.

THE GNOME OF THE HILLOCK	133

"He enter'd, but he enter'd full of wrath,
His flaming robes stream'd out beyond his heels,
And gave a roar."—*Hyperion.*

THE BHEESTY'S MOTHER	142

"I beheld where the Ancient of Days did sit, whose hair on his head was like the pure wool."—*Daniel.*

"A withered old beldame, too poor to keep a cat, hurkling on her hunkers over a feeble fire of sticks."—*Christopher North.*

THE FAQUIR	145

"In his eyes the foreknowledge of death."—*Swinburne.*

THE GARDEN OF KHUSRU	150

THE SYCE'S CHILDREN	154

"The Italians make little difference between children and nephews or near kinsfolk; but so they be of the same lump they care not."—*Bacon's Essays.*

Mosquitoes 160

"With drowsy song
The grey-fly wound his sullen horn along."
Childhood (*Kirke White*).
"The grey-fly winds her sultry horn."—*Lycidas* (*Milton*).

Part IV.

UNDER THE TREES.

Under the Tamarind 167
Under the Mango 175
Under the Peepul 184
Under the Bamboos 193
Under the Banyan 202

Part I.

IN MY INDIAN GARDEN.

THE BIRDS.
OF HENS.
CORVUS SPLENDENS.
GREEN PARROTS.
THE MYNAS.
THE SEVEN SISTERS.
THE MUNGOOSE.
THE GREY SQUIRREL.
THE ANTS.
THE PARIAH DOG AND THE CAT.
THE PEA-BOY.
THE FRUITS.
THE FROGS.

IN MY INDIAN GARDEN.

THE BIRDS.

A GARDEN everywhere is to the natural world beyond its walls very much what a good Review number is to the rest of literature. Shrubs and flowers, indigenous or of distant derivation, jumbled together, attract an equally miscellaneous congregation of birds and insects, and by their fresher leaves, brighter blossoms, or juicier fruit, detain for a time the capricious and fastidious visitors. And an Indian Garden is *par excellence* Nature's museum—a gallery of curiosities for the indifferent to admire, the interested to study. It is a Travellers' Club, an Œcumenical Council, a Parliament of buzzing, humming, chirping, and chattering things. The earth beneath, the trees between, and the air above, are full of busy life for all who have eyes to see, ears to hear, or the will to learn of the curious humanity of beasts and birds and little insects.

In my Indian Garden.

The great unclouded sky is terraced out by flights of birds. Here, in the region of trees, church-spires, and house-tops, flutter and have their being the myriad tribes who plunder while they share the abodes of men; the diverse crew who jostle on the earth, the lowest level of creation, with mammals, and walk upon its surface plantigrade; the small birds whose names children learn, whom school-boys snare, and who fill the shelves of museums as the Insessores, or birds that perch. They are the commonalty of birddom, who furnish forth the mobs which bewilder the drunken-flighted jay when he jerks, shrieking in a series of blue hyphen-flashes through the air, or which, when some owlet as unfortunate as foolish has let itself be jostled from its cosy hole beneath the thatch out into the glare of daylight, crowd round the blinking stranger and unkindly jeer it from amongst them. These are the ground-floor tenants, our every-day walk acquaintances, who look up to crows as to Members of Council, and think no mean thing of green parrots. And yet there are among them many of a notable plumage and song, more indeed than among the upper ten of Volucres, just as, if the Indian proverb goes for aught, there are more pretty women among the lowest, the *mehter*, than any other caste. On the second floor, where nothing but clear ether checks their flight, swim the great eagles, the knightly falcons and the vultures, grand when on their wide, loose pinions they float and circle—sordid only, like the gods of old, when they stoop to earth. These divide the peerage of the skies, and among them is universal a fine purity of colour and form—a nobility of power. They are all princes among the feathered, gentle and graceful as they wheel and re-curve undisturbed in their own high domains, but fierce in battle and terribly swift when they shoot down to earth, their keen vision covering half a province, their cruel cry shrilling to the floors of heaven. See them now, with no quarry to pursue, no battle to fight, and mark the exceeding beauty of their motion. In tiers above each other, the shrill-voiced kites, their sharp-cut wings bent into a bow, their tail, a third wing almost, spread out fanwise to the wind—the vultures parallel, but wheeling in higher spheres on level pinions—the hawk, with his strong bold flight, smiting his way up to the highest place; while far above him, where the sky-roof is cobwebbed with white clouds, float dim specks, which in the distance seem hardly moving — the sovereign eagles. They can stare at the sun without blinking; we cannot, so let us turn our eyes lower—to the garden level. Pleasant indeed is my Indian Garden. Here in a green colonnade stand the mysterious broad-leaved plantains with their strange spikes of fruit—there the dark mango. In a grove together the spare-leaved peepul, that sacred yet treacherous tree that drags down the humble shrine which it was placed to sanctify; the shapely tamarind, with its clouds of foliage; the graceful neem; the patulous teak, with its great leathern leaves, and the

In my Indian Garden.

bamboos the tree-cat loves. Below them grow a wealth of roses, the lavender-blossomed durantas, the cactus grotesque in growth, the poyntzettia with its stars of scarlet, the spiky aloes, the sick-scented jessamine, and the quaint coral-trees; while over all shoots up the palm. The citron, lime, and orange-trees are beautiful alike when they load the air with the perfume of their waxen flowers, or when they are snowing their sweet petals about them, or when heavy-fruited they trail their burdened branches to rest their yellow treasure on the ground.

OF HENS.

AND pleasant is it to see the <u>garden's visitors</u>. The crow pheasant stalks past with his chestnut wings drooping by his side, the magpie with his curious <u>dreamland note</u> climbs the tree overhead, the woodpeckers flutter the creviced ants, the sprightly bulbul tunes his throat with crest erect, the glistening flower-pecker haunts the lilies, the oriole flashes in the splendour of his golden plumage from tree to tree, the bee-eater slides through the air, the doves call to each other from the shady guava grove, the poultry—Poultry? Yes, they do not, it is true, strictly appertain to gardens, but rather to hen-houses and stable-yards, to the outskirts of populous places and the remoter corners of cultivated fields. Yet they are—and that not seldom—to be found and met with in gardens where, if ill-conditioned, they do not scruple to commit an infinity of damage by looking inquisitively, albeit without judgment, after food, at the roots of plants, and by making for themselves comfortable hollows in the conspicuous corners of flower-beds, wherein, with a notable assiduity, they sit to ruffle their feathers during the early hours of sunshine. These pastimes are not, however, without some hazard to the hens, for thereby they render themselves both obnoxious to mankind and noticeable by their other enemies. A cat who has two minds about attacking a fowl when in a decent posture and enjoying herself as a hen should do, does not hesitate to assault her when met with in a dust-hole, her feathers all set the wrong way and in an ecstasy of titillation. A kite will swoop from the blue to see what manner of eatable she may be, nor when she is laying bare the roots of a rose-bush is the gardener reluctant to stone her, whereby the hen is caused some personal inconvenience and much mental perturbation, determining her to escape (always, let it be noticed, in the wrong direction) with the greatest possible precipitancy. These same hens are, I think, the most foolish of fowls—for on this point the popular proverb that makes a goose to be a fool is in error, as the goose is in reality one of the most cunning of birds, even in a domestic state, while in a wild state there are few birds to compare with them for vigilance. The hen, however, is an extraordinary fool, and in no circumstance of life does she behave with a seemly composure. Should a bird pass overhead, she immediately concludes that it is about to fall upon her head; while if she hears any sound for which she cannot satisfactorily account to herself, she sets up a woeful clucking, in which, after a few

Of Hens. 9

rounds, she is certain to be joined by her comrades, who foregather with her to cluck and croon, though they have not even her excuse of having heard the original noise. But their troubles are many.

Life is many-sided. Indeed, you may examine it from so many standpoints that had you even the hundred eyes of Argus, and each eye hundred-faceted like the orb of a dragon-fly, you could not be a master of the subject "from all sides." And yet how often does the man who has surveyed his neighbours from two points only—the bottom of the ladder and the top—affect to have exhausted the experience of life. For Man to dogmatize wisely on this life is to argue simplicity in it.

For instance, have you ever looked at life from the standpoint of a dâk-bungalow[1] fowl? Perhaps not, but it is instructive nevertheless as exemplifying the reciprocity of brain and body, and showing how one trait of character by exaggerated development may develope and exaggerate certain features physical as well as mental, obliterate others, and leave the owner as skeletonized in mind in body. *Suspicion* is the fungus that, taking root in the mind of the dâk-bungalow fowl, strangles all its finer feelings (though fostering self-reliance), and makes miserable by its gigantic growth the bird's daily life. Think of the lives cursed by suspicion, and confer your pity on the hen. Cromwell shifting from bedroom to bedroom, and the royal Louis refusing food. Adam Smith was

[1] Staging-house.

stolen n infancy by gipsies, and his parents lived ever afterwards in terror for the rest of their children. Vulcan, suspicious of his wife's friends, gave her, so Burton says, creaking shoes; but his life, in spite of precautions, must have been a weary one. There was Mars coming in every morning to flirt with the Paphian on the flimsy pretence of seeing how the lame forge-man was getting on with his new greaves (as soon as one job was finished another order was given), and while on the anvil the strokes rang evenly, Venus was in the parlour slipping off her shoes. But what was this compared to the life of the dâk-bungalow fowl? His whole life is spent in strategy. For him every advance in his direction is a wile, each corner an ambuscade, and each conclave of servants a cabal. With every sun comes a Rye House Plot for the wretched bird, and before evening he has had to run the gauntlet of a Vehm-gericht. His brother, suspicious yet all too confiding, would trust no one but the wife of the grain-dealer who lived at the corner—and this single confidence cost him his life. So our bird trusts no one—certainly not the Tarpeia-Jael-Judith-Dalila at the corner of the road.

Indeed, now that I come myself to think seriously of the dâk-bungalow fowl, I would not hesitate to say that the washerman's donkey has a better life than it. The donkey can remember childhood's years as an interval of frivolity and lightheartedness, and even in maturer life it is free (with three of its legs) after the day's work is over to disport itself with its kind. But the case is different with the bird. Pullets of the tenderest years are sought out for broth; adolescence is beset with peril in hardly a less degree than puberty; while, alas! old age itself is not respected. The value of life depends, I fancy, upon the amount of game obtained for the candle burnt; or, supposing pleasure to be a negative quantity, upon the amount of unpleasantness avoided during life. And looking at it from either point of view, I am inclined to think the value of life to a dâk-bungalow fowl must be very trifling. Like Japanese youth it lives with sudden death ever in prospect, but the hara-kiri in the case of the fowl is not an honourable termination of life, while the lively apprehension of it unwholesomely sharpens its vigilance. It has, moreover, nothing to live on and plenty of it; and this diet affects its physique, inasmuch as it prevents the increase of flesh, while the constant evasion of death developes its muscles—the thigh-bones assuming vulturine dimensions. The feathers, by frequent escapings through small holes, become ragged and irregular, the tail is systematically discarded as being dangerous and a handle to ill-wishers. Death therefore must come upon some of them as a sharp cure for life— *il est mort guéri.* But to others it is the bitter end of a life of perilous pleasures—to such a one perhaps as the following. The bird I speak of was a fine young cock, a Nazarene in his unclipt wings, with the columnar legs of an athlete, snatching life by sheer pluck and dying without disgrace. His death happened in this wise. There came up the hill one day some travellers with whom the cook at the staging-house wished to stand well, and when they asked, "What is there to eat?" he replied with suavity, "Whatever your honours choose to order." So they ordered beef and then mutton, but there being neither they desisted from "ordering," and left it to the cook to arrange their meal. And he gave them soup made of an infant poult, two side-dishes composed of two elder brothers, *a fine fowl roasted by way of joint*, and the grandmother of the family furnished forth a curry. And one of the party watched the dinner being caught. With the soup there was little difficulty, for it succumbed to a most obvious fraud. The side-dishes fell victims to curiosity, for while they were craning their necks into the cook-room door, a hand came suddenly round the corner and closed upon them. The curry, poor old soul, was taken in her afternoon sleep. But the roast, the bird particularized above, showed sport, as well it might. For seven months it had daily evaded death, scorning alike the wiles of the cook and the artifices of his minions. Nothing would tempt it during the day within the enclosure in which so many of its family had lost their lives, and as it roosted high up in the walnut-tree behind the bungalow, night surprises were out of the question. Whenever travellers came in sight it would either fly on to the roof of the bungalow, and thence survey the preparations for dinner; or slipping away quietly over the cliff would enjoy healthful ease in some sequestered nook, whither was borne, tempered by distance and the comfortable sense of security, the last screech of the less wary. But its day had come. The fig-tree had drunk of the Neda. *The travellers had been expected.* An hour, therefore, before they came in sight preparations were made for the great capture, and when on the appearance of the first horseman the fowl turned as usual to escape, he found two boys on the roof of the bungalow, six more up the walnut-tree, and a cordon of men round the yard. There was nothing for it but to trust to his wings; so mounting on the wall he flew for his life. And his strong wings bore him bravely—up over the fowl-yard and the goat-house, and the temple, over the upturned faces of the shouting men—up into the unbroken sky. Below him, far, far down he saw the silver thread of water that lay along the valley between the hills. But there was a worse enemy than man on the watch—a hungry eagle. And on a sudden our flier saw between him and the red sunset the king of birds in kingly flight towards him, and stopping himself in his course he came fluttering down— poor Icarus!—to the friendly covert of earth with outspread wings. But the eagle with closed pinions fell like a thunder-bolt plumb from out of the heavens, and striking him in mid-sky sent him twirling earthward; then swooping down again grasped him in his yellow talons before he touched the ground, and rising with slow flight winged his burdened way to the nearest resting-place—the roof of the dâk bungalow! But his exploit had been watched, and hardly had his feet touched the welcome tiles before a shower of sticks and stones rained round him. One pebble struck him, and rising hastily at the affront, his prey escaped his talons, and rolling over and over down the roof fell into the arms of the exultant cook! But the scream of the baffled eagle drowned the death-cry of the fowl.

CORVUS SPLENDENS.

CORVUS SPLENDENS is the scientific name given by Vieillot to that "treble-dated bird," the common crow of India, and although one naturalist yearned to change it to "shameless" (*impudicus*), and although another still declares that *splendens* is inappropriate, and tends to bring scientific nomenclature into ridicule, that bird—as was only to be expected from a crow—has kept its mendacious adjective, and in spite of Hodgson and Jerdon is still, in name, as fine a bird in India as it was time out of mind in Olympus. *Splendens* or not at present, the crow must have had recommendations either of mind or person to have been chosen, as Ovid tells us it was, as the messenger-bird of so artistic a deity as Apollo. But the crow lost Paradise—and good looks with it—not for one impulsive act, but for a fortnight's hard sinning. Now punishment has a hardening influence on some people, and it has had a most dreadful effect on the corvine disposition. Heedless of all moral obligations, gluttonous, and a perverter of truth, Ovid tells us it was, even in its best days; but now it has developed into a whole legion of devilry. Lest a Baboo should think to trip me up by throwing Menu in my teeth and quoting from the great lawgiver "A good wife should be like a crow," I would give it as my opinion that Menu, when he said this, referred to that doubtful virtue of the crow that forbids any exhibition of conjugal tenderness before the public eye—an unnatural instinct and reserve, to my thinking. Crows cannot, like young sweeps, be called "innocent blacknesses," for their nigritude is the livery of sin, the badge of crime, like the scarlet V on the shoulder of the convict *voleur*, the dark brand on Cain's brow, the snow-white leprosy of Gehazi, or the yellow garb of Norfolk Islanders. And yet they do not wear their colour with humility or even common decency. They swagger in it, pretending they chose that exact shade for themselves. Did they not do this, perhaps Jerdon would not have begrudged them their flattering name, nor Hodgson have called them "*impudicos*," but by their effrontery they have raised every man's hand against them; and were they anything but crows, they must have had to take, like Ishmael the son of Hagar, to the desert. Perhaps it is that they presume upon their past honours. If so, they should beware. Cole's dog was too proud to move out of the way of a cart of manure, and Southey has told us his fate. Again, their Greek and Latin glories have had a serious counterpoise in the writings of modern ancients, where the nature of crows is proven as swart as their Ethiop faces. Is it not written in the Singhalese Pratyasataka that nothing can improve a crow? Students of Burton will remember that in the *Anatomy of Melancholy* devils (including sprites and such like devilkins) are divided into nine classes; for though Bodine declared that all devils must of necessity be spherical in shape, perfect rounds, his theory we are expressly told was quashed by Zaminchus, who proved that they assume divers forms, "sometimes those of cats and crows." Zaminchus was doubtless right, and no one, therefore, should feel any tenderness for these shreds of Satan, these cinders from Tartarus. Zaminchus superfluously adds that in these forms they are "more knowing than any human being" (*quovis homine scientior*), and another old writer just as needlessly tells us that these "terrestrial devils" are in the habit of " flapping down platters" and "making strange noises." Some, however, may urge that because some crows are devils, it does not follow that all are. This is plausible, but unworthy of the subject, which should be studied in a liberal spirit and without hair-splitting. When King John killed Jews, he didn't first finically investigate if they were usurers—he knew they were Jews, and that was enough. Besides, did any one ever see a crow that was not "*quovis homine scientior*"? If he did, he proved it by putting it to death, and, as dead crows count for nothing, that individual bird cannot be cited as a case in point.

Further, do not all crows "flap down platters" (when they get the chance) and "make strange noises"? Are not these unequivocal signs of bedevilment? Do not Zaminchus, Bustius, and Cardan agree on this point? Does not the old Chinese historian lay it down that in the south of Sweden is situate "the land of crows and demons"? Is there not in Norway a fearful hill called Huklebrig, whither and whence fiery chariots are commonly seen by the country people carrying to and fro the souls of bad men in the likeness of crows? Crows, then, are indubitably the connecting link between devils Class 3, "inventors of all mischief," Prince Belial at their head,—and Class 4, "malicious devils," under Prince Asmodeus.[1] An inkling of their fallen state seems to be floating in the cerebra of crows, for they sin naturally and never beg pardon. Did any one ever see a contrite and repentant crow? When taken *flagrante delicto*, does this nobody's child provoke commiseration by craven and abject postures, deprecating anger by looks of penitence? Quite the contrary. These birds, if put to it, would deny that they stole Cicero's pillow when he was dying, or that they sate, the abomination of desolation, where they ought not—profaning the Teraphim of John de Montfort, insulting his household gods and desecrating his Penates, while in the next room that great soldier and statesman was receiving the last con-

---

[1] I have here preferred to adopt Burton's classification.—P. R.

solations of Extreme Unction? Yet it is known they did. They tread the earth as if they had been always of it. And yet it pleases me to remember how Indra, in wrath for their tale-bearing—for had they not carried abroad the secrets of the Councils of the Gods?—hurled the brood down through all the hundred stages of his Heaven. Petruchio thought it hard to be braved in his own house by a tailor, and the tailor by an elephant; how keenly either would have felt the familiarity of Indian crows! In the verandahs they parade the reverend sable which they disgrace; they walk in the odour of sanctity through open doors sleek as Chadband, wily as Pecksniff. Their step is grave, and they ever seem on the point of quoting Scripture, while their eyes are wandering on carnal matters. Like Stiggins, they keep a sharp look-out for tea-time. They hanker after flesh-pots. They are as chary of their persons as the bamboo of its blossom, and distant to strangers. In England they pretend to be rooks (except during rook-shooting), but in India they brazen it out upon their own infamous individuality—for there are no rooks.

GREEN PARROTS.

CERVANTES has recorded the fact that Theophrastus complained " of the long life given to crows." Now the argument of this complaint is not so superficial as at first it seems, and really contains internal evidence of a knowledge of bird-nature. Theophrastus, I take it grumbled not simply because crows did in a long life get through more mischief than other birds can in a shorter one, but because, if Atropos were only more impartially nimble with her shears, crows would never be able to get through any mischief at all. And in this lies a great point of difference between the sombre crow and the dædal parrot. The crow requires much time to develope and perfect his misdemeanours ; the parrot brings his mischiefs to market in the green leaf. The first is a crafty, calculating villain ; the latter a headlong blackguard. While a crow will spend a week with a view to the ultimate abstraction of a key, the parrot will have scrambled and screeched in a day through a cycle of larcenous gluttonies, and before the crow has finished reconnoitring the gardener, the parrot has stripped the fruit-tree. From these differences in the characters of the birds I hold that Theophrastus chose "crows" advisedly, and made his complaint with judgment; but I wonder that, having thus headed a list of grievances, he did not continue it with a protest against the green colour given to parrots. The probable explanation of the oversight is, that he never saw a Green Parrot. But we who *do* see them have surely a reasonable cause for complaint, when nature creates thieves and then gives them a passport to impunity. For the green parrot has a large brain (some naturalists would like to see the Psittacid family on this account rank first among birds), and he knows that he is green as well as we do, and knowing it he makes the most of nature's injudicious gift. He settles with a screech among your mangoes, and as you approach, the phud! phud! of the falling fruitlings assures you that he is not gone. But where is he? Somewhere in the tree you may be sure, probably with an unripe fruit in his claw, which is raised half way to his beak, but certainly with a round black eye fixed on you, for, while you are straining to distinguish green feathers from green leaves, he breaks with a sudden rush through the foliage, on the other side of the tree, and is off in an apotheosis of screech to his watch-tower on a distant tree. To give the parrot his due, however, we must remember that he did not choose his own colour,—it was thrust upon him; and we must further allow that, snob as he is, he possesses certain manly virtues. He is wanting in neither personal courage, assurance, nor promptitude, but he abuses these virtues by using them in the service of vice. Moreover, he is a glutton, and, unlike his neighbours, the needle of his thoughts and endeavours always points towards his stomach. The starlings, bigots to a claim which they have forged to the exclusive ownership of the croquet ground, divide their attention for a moment between worms and intruders. The kite forbears to flutter the dove-cotes while he squeals his love-song to his mate; the hawk now and again affords healthy excitement to a score of crows who keck at him as he flaps unconcerned on his wide, ragged wings through the air. "Opeechee the robin" has found a bird smaller than himself, and is accordingly pursuing it relentlessly through bush and brier; the thinly-feathered babblers are telling each other the secret of a mungoose being at that moment in the water-pipe; while the squirrels, sticking head downwards to their respective branches, are having a twopenny-halfpenny argument across the garden path. Meanwhile, the green parrot is desolating the fruit-tree. Like the Ettrick Shepherd they never can eat *a few* of anything, and his luncheons are all heavy dinners. "That frugal bit of the old Britons of the bigness of a bean," which could satisfy the hunger and thirst of our ancestors for a whole day, would not suffice the green parrot for one meal, for not only is his appetite inordinate, but his wastefulness also, and what he cannot eat he destroys. He enters a tree of fruit as the Visigoths entered a building. His motto is, "What I cannot take I will not leave," and he pillages the branches, gutting them of even their unripest fruit. Dr. Jerdon, in his *Birds of India*, records the fact that "owls attack these birds by night," and there is, ill-feeling apart, certainly something very comfortable in the knowledge, that while we are warm a-bed owls are most probably garrotting the green parrots.

THE MYNAS.

I HAVE spoken elsewhere, with some inadvertence, of "the Republic of Birds," although by my own showing—for I write of "sovereign" eagles and the "knightly" falcons—the constitution of the volucrine world is an unlimited monarchy, of which the despotism is only tempered by the strong social bonds that lend strength to the lower orders of birds. The tyrant kite is powerless before the corvine Vehmgericht; and it is with hesitation that the hawk offers violence to a sparrows' club. But there are undoubtedly among the feathered race some to whom a Republic would present itself as the more perfect form of government, and to none more certainly than the Mynas.[1] The myna is, although a moderate, a very decided republican, for sober in mind as in apparel, he sets his face against such vain frivolities as the tumbling of pigeons, the meretricious

---

[1] *Sturninæ*, the Starlings.

dancing of peafowl, and the gaudy bedizenment of the minivets, holding that life is real, life is earnest, and, while worms are to be found beneath the grass, to be spent in serious work. To quote "ane aunciente clerke," he "obtests against the chaunting of foolish litanies before the idols of one's own conceit," would "chase away all bewildering humours and fancies;" and would say with the clerke "that, though the cautelous tregœtour, or, as the men of France do call him, the jongleur, doth make a very pretty play with two or three balls which seem to live in the air, and which do not depart from him, yet I would rather, after our old English fashion, have the ball tossed from hand to hand, or that one should propulse the ball against the little guichet while another should repel it with the batting staff. This I hold to be the fuller exercise." The myna therefore views with some displeasure the dilettante hawking of bee-eaters and the leisurely deportment of the crow-pheasant, cannot be brought to see the utility of the luxurious hoopoe's crest, and loses all patience with the köel-cuckoo for his idle habit of spending his forenoons in tuning his voice. For the patient kingfisher he entertains a moderate respect, and he holds in esteem the industrious woodpecker; but the scapegrace parrot is an abomination to him, and, had he the power, the myna would altogether exterminate the race of humming-birds for their persistent trifling over lilies. Life with him is all work, and he makes it, as Souvestre says, "a legal process." Of course he has a wife, and she celebrates each anniversary of spring by presenting him with a nestful of young mynas, but her company rather subdues and sobers him than makes him frivolous or giddy, for as the myna is, his wife is—of one complexion of feather and mind. A pair of mynas (for these discreet birds are seldom seen except in pairs) remind one of a Dutch burgher and his frau. They are comfortably dressed, well fed, of a grave deportment, and so respectable that scandal hesitates to whisper their name. In the empty babble of the Seven Sisters, the fruitless controversies of finches, the bickerings of amatory sparrows (every sparrow is at heart a rake), or the turmoil of kites, they take no part—holding aloof alike from the monarchical exclusiveness of the jealous Raptores and the democrat communism of crows. The gourd will not climb on the olive, and the olive-tree, it is said, will not grow near the oak. Between the grape of story and the cabbage there is a like antipathy, "and everlasting hate the vine to ivy bears." The apple detests the walnut "whose malignant touch impairs all generous fruit." So with the myna. It shrinks from the neighbourhood of the strong, and resents the companionship of the humble. But among vegetables, if there is antipathy there is also sympathy; for does not the Latin poet say that the elm loves the vine? country folk declare that the fig grows best near rue, and the legend ballad of the Todas tells us how the cachew apple droops when the cinnamon dies.

But among the mynas there is no such profligacy or tenderness, and over the annihilation of the whole world of birds they would be even such "pebble stones" as Launce's dog. At the same time they are not intrusive with their likes and dislikes. If the squirrel chooses to chirrup all day, they let him do so, and they offer no opposition to the ostentatious combats of robins. Nor do they trespass on their neighbours with idle curiosity. That butterflies should mysteriously migrate in great clouds, moving against the wind across wide waters, and even tempt the ocean itself with nothing more definite than the horizon before them as a resting-place, may set the inquisitive crow thinking, or furnish Humboldt with matter for long conjecturing; but the mynas would express no surprise at the phenomenon. They waste no time wondering with others why the wagtail so continuously wags its tail, nor would they vex the Syrian coney with idle questions as to its preference for rocky places. Such things have set others a-thinking, and would make the leaf-loving squirrel silly with surprise; but the Essene myna!—"Let the world revolve," he says; "we are here to work, and, in the name of the Prophet—*worms.*" He comes of a race of poor antecedents, and has no lineage worth boasting of. The crow has Greek and Latin memories, and for the antiquity of the sparrow we have the testimony of Holy Writ. It is true that in the stories of India the myna has frequent and honourable mention; but the authors speak of the hill-bird—a notable fowl with strange powers of mimicry, and always a favourite with the people—and not the homely Quaker bird, who so diligently searches our grass-plots, and may be seen, from dawn to twilight, busy at his appointed work, the consumption of little grubs. The lust of the green parrot for orchard brigandage, or of the proud-stomached king-crow for battle with his kind, are as whimsical caprices, fancies of the moment, when compared to the steady assiduity with which this Puritan bird pursues the object of his creation. And the result is that the myna has no wit. Like the Germans, he is incomparable at hard, unshowy work, but they, as one, a wit himself, has said of them, are "only moderately mirthful in their humour." Intelligence is his of a high order, for, busy as he may be, the myna descries before all others the far-away speck in the sky which will grow into a hawk, and it is from the myna's cry of alarm that the garden becomes first aware of the danger that is approaching. But wit he has none. His only way of catching a worm is to lay hold of its tail and pull it out of its hole—generally breaking it in the middle, and losing the bigger half. He does not tap the ground as the wryneck will tap the tree, to stimulate the insect to run out to be eaten entire, nor like the stork imitate a dead thing, till the frog, tired of waiting for him to move, puts his head above the green pond. "To strange mysterious dulness still the friend" he parades the croquet lawn, joins in grave converse with another by the roadside, or sits to exchange ignorance with an acquaintance on a rail. At night the mynas socially congregate together; and, with a clamour quite unbecoming their character, make their arrangements for the night, contending for an absolute equality even in sleep.

Has it ever struck you how fortunate it is for the world of birds that of the twenty-four hours some are passed in darkness? And yet without the protection of night the earth would be assuredly depopulated of small birds, and the despots, whom the mynas detest, would be left alone to contest in internecine conflict the dominion of the air.

THE SEVEN SISTERS.[1]

AS busy as the mynas, but less silent in their working, are those sad-coloured birds hopping about in the dust and incessantly talking while they hop. They are called by the natives "The Seven Sisters," and seem to have always some little difference on hand to settle. But if they gabble till the coming of the Coquecigrues they will never settle it. Fighting? Not at all; do not be misled by the tone of voice. That heptachord clamour is not the expression of any strong feelings. It is only a way they have. They always exchange their commonplaces as if their next neighbour was out of hearing. If they could but be quiet they might pass for the bankers among the birds. They look so very respectable. But though they dress so soberly, their behaviour is unseemly. The Prince in Herodotus' history disappointed the expectations of his friends by dancing head downwards on a table, "gesticulating with his legs." If Coleridge's wise-looking friend had preserved his silence

[1] The Babbler-thrushes, *Malacocircus.*-

through the whole meal, the poet would have remembered him as one of the most intelligent men of his acquaintance; but the apple dumplings making him speak burst the bubble of his reputation. His speech bewrayed him, like the Shibboleth at the ford of Jordan, the "bread and cheese" of the Fleming persecution, or the Galilean twang of the impetuous saint. Pythagoreans may, if they will, aver that these birds are the original masons and hodmen of Babel, but I would rather believe that in a former state they were old Hindu women, garrulous [2] and addicted to raking about amongst rubbish heaps—as all old native women seem to be. The Seven Sisters pretend to feed on insects, but that is only when they cannot get peas. Look at them now! The whole family, a septemvirate of sin, among your Marrowfat peas, gobbling and gabbling as if they believed in Dr. Cumming. And it is of no use to expel them—for they will return, and

> "Often scared,
> As oft return: a pert voracious kind."

When it is night they will go off with a great deal of preliminary talk to their respective boarding-houses, for these birds, though at times as quarrelsome as Sumatrans during the pepper harvest, are sociable and lodge together. The weak point of this arrangement is that often a bird—perhaps the middle one of a long row of closely-

---

[2] "Ten measures of garrulity," says the Talmud, "came down from heaven, and the women took nine of them."

packed snoozers—has a bad dream, or loses his balance, and instantly the shock flashes along the line. The whole dormitory blazes up at once with indignation, and much bad language is bandied about promiscuously in the dark. The abusive shower at length slackens, and querulous monosyllables and indistinct animal noises take the place of the septemfluous (Fuller has sanctified the word) vituperation, when some individual, tardily exasperate at the unseemly din, lifts up his voice in remonstrance, and rekindles the smouldering fire. Sometimes he suddenly breaks off—suggesting to a listener the idea that his next neighbour had silently kicked him —but more often the mischief is irreparable, and the din runs its course, again dwindles away, and is again relit, perhaps more than once before all heads are safely again under wing.

THE MUNGOOSE.

AS a contrast to the fidgetty birds, glance your eye along the garden path and take note of that pink-nosed mungoose[1] gazing placidly out of the water-pipe. It looks as shy as Oliver Twist before the Board; but that is only because it sees no chance of being able to chase you about, catch you and eat you. If you were a snake or a lizard you would find it provokingly familiar, and as brisk as King Ferdinand at an *auto-da-fé:* for the scent of a lively snake is to the mungoose as pleasant as that of valerian to cats, attar to a Begum, aniseed to pigeons, or burning Jews to His Most Catholic Majesty aforementioned; and when upon the war-trail the mungoose is as different to the every day animal as the Sunday gentleman in the Park in green gloves and a blue necktie is to the obsequious young man who served you across the counter on Saturday. Usually, the mungoose is to be seen slinking timorously along the

[1] The Ichneumon, *Viverrina*.

narrow watercourses or, under cover of the turf edge, gliding along to some hunting-ground among the aloes, whence if it unearths a quarry it will emerge with its fur on end and its tail like a bottle-brush, its eyes dancing in its head, and all its body agog with excitement,—reckless of the dead leaves crackling as it scuttles after the flying reptile,—flinging itself upon the victim with a zest and single-mindedness wonderful to see. That pipe is its city of refuge—the asylum in all times of trouble, to which it betakes itself when annoyed by the cat who lives in the carrot-bed, or the bird-boy who by his inhuman cries greatly perplexes the robins in the peas, or when its nerves have been shaken by the sudden approach of the silent-footed gardener or by a *rencontre* with the long-tailed pariah dog that lives in the outer dust. The mungoose, although his own brothers in Nepal have the same smell in a worse degree, is the sworn foe of musk-rats. "All is not mungoose that smells of musk," it reasons as it follows up the trail of its chitt-chittering victim; but although it enjoys this "le sport," it sometimes essays the less creditable battue. Jerdon says, "It is very destructive to such birds as frequent the ground. Not unfrequently it gets access to tame pigeons, rabbits, or poultry, and commits great havoc, sucking the blood only of several." He adds that he has "often seen it make a dash into a verandah where caged birds were placed and endeavour to tear them from their cages." The mungoose family, in fact, do duty for weasels, and if game were preserved in India would be vermin. Even at present some of the blame so lavishly showered on the tainted musk-rat might be transferred to the mungoose. A little more of that same blame might perhaps be made over to another popular favourite, the grey squirrel.

THE GREY SQUIRREL.

THE Palm Squirrel, as it is more properly called, will come into a room and eat the fruit on your sideboard, or into a vinery and incontinently borrow your grapes. A rat-trap in such cases may do some good, but a complete cure is hopeless. Nothing but the Arminian doctrine of universal grace will save the squirrel from eternal damnation, for its presumption is unique. The plummet of reflection cannot sound it, nor the net of memory bring up a precedent. It is gratuitous, unprovoked, and aimless. It is all for love. There are no stakes such as the crow plays for, and in its shrill gamut there is no string of menace or of challenge. Its scrannel quips are pointless—so let them pass. Any one, unless he be a Scotch piper, has a right to stone the Seven Sisters for their fulsome clatter, but the tongue of the squirrel is free as air. There is no embargo on it—it is out of bond, and wags when and where it lists. Let the craven kite (itself the butt of smaller birds) swoop

The Grey Squirrel.

at it, but give your sympathy to the squirrel. A woman who cannot kiss, and a bird which cannot sing, ought to be at any rate taught; but who would look for harmony from a squirrel? Was wisdom ever found in Gotham or truth in the compliments of beggars? Would you hook Leviathan by the nose, or hedge a cuckoo in? Again, besides its voice, people have been found to object to its tail. But Hiawatha liked it. There is no malice in the motion of a squirrel's tail. It does not resemble the cocked-up gesture of the robin's or the wren's. It doesn't swing like the cat's, or dart like the scorpion's. It is never offensively straight on end like a cow's on a windy day, nor slinking like a pariah dog's. It has none of the odious mobility of the monkey's, nor the three-inch arrogance of the goat's. Neither is there in it the pendulous monotony of the wag-tail's, nor the spasmodic wriggle of the sucking lamb's. Yet it is a speaking feature. That fluffy perkiness is an index of the squirrel mind. With an upward jerk it puts a question, with a downward one emphasizes an assertion; gives plausibility with a wave, and stings with sarcasm in a series of disconnected lilts—for the squirrel is as inquisitive as Empedocles, as tediously emphatic as the Ephesians, and in self-confidence a Crœsus. It would not have hesitated to suggest to Solomon solutions to the Queen of Sheba's conundrums, nor to volunteer likely answers to the riddle of the Sphinx. It is impervious to jibes. Scoffs and derision are thrown away upon it as much as solid argument. Hard names do it no hurt. It would not be visibly affected if you called it a parallelopiped, or the larva of a marine Ascidian. Perhaps it is a philosopher, for, since squirrels dropped their nutshells on Primeval Man, no instance is on record of a melancholy squirrel. Its emotions (precipitate terror excepted) are shallow, and though it may be tamed, will form no strong attachments; while its worldly wisdom is great. Like the frog in Æsop, it is "extreme wise." Given a three-inch post, the squirrel can always keep out of sight. You may go round and round, but it will always be "on the other side."

THE ANTS.

SQUIRRELS excepted, the most prominent members of Indian garden life are ants, for they stamp their broad-arrow everywhere; their advertisements may be read on almost every tree trunk, and samples of their work seen on all the paths. They have a head office in most verandahs, with branch establishments in the bath-rooms, while their agents are ubiquitous, laying earth-heaps wherever they travel —each heap the outward and visible sign of much inward tunnelling, and which, towards the end of the rainy season, will fall in. Engineering seems to be their favourite profession although some have a passion for plastering, and when other surfaces fail will lay a coat of mud on the level ground, for the after-pleasure of creeping under it. Others are bigots to geographical dis covery, and are constantly wandering into dangerous places, whence they escape only by a series of miracles. Of some a pastoral life is all the joy, for they keep herds

of green aphides—better known as "blight"—which
they milk regularly for the sake of the sweet leaf-juice
they secrete. Others, again, are hunters and live on the
produce of the chase. They organize foraging parties
and issue forth a host of Lilliputians to drag home a
Brobdignag cricket, or, marshalled on the war-trail, file
out to plunder the larders of their neighbours. The
bulk, however, are omnivorous and jacks-of-all-trades,
with a decided leaning towards vegetable food and ex-
cavation; and it is in this, the enormous consumption
of seeds in the ant nurseries, that this family contributes
its quota to the well-being of creation, a quota which
after all scarcely raises it, in point of usefulness, to the
level of butterflies and moths—popularly supposed to be
the idlest and least useful of created insects. It ought,
however, to be kept in mind that butterflies are only
beatified caterpillars, and when we see them flying about,
should remember that their work is over and they are
enjoying their vacation. They have been raised to the
Upper House. From being laborious managers they
have become the sleeping partners in a thriving business.
While they were caterpillars they worked hard and well;
so Nature, to reward them, dresses them up to look at-
tractive, and sends them out as butterflies—to get married.
The ants, on the other hand, did no work when they
were grubs, so they have to do a good deal in their
maturity. They have to provide food for successive
broods of hungry youngsters, who, when grown up, will

join them in feeding their younger brothers and sisters; or, if they are of the favoured few, will enter ant-life with wings and be blown away by the wind a few hundred yards, to become the founders of new colonies. The actual balance of work done by caterpillars and ants, respectively, is indeed about equal; the only difference being, that caterpillars check vegetation by feeding themselves, and ants by feeding their babies, while the balance of mischief done is very much against the ants. The commonest of all the Indian ants, or at any rate the most conspicuous, are the black ones, to be found marauding on every side-board, and whose normal state seems to be one of criminal trespass. These from their size are perhaps also the most interesting, as it requires little exertion to distinguish between the classes of individuals that in the aggregate make up "a nest of ants." There is the blustering "soldier" or "policeman" ant, who goes about wagging his great head and snapping his jaws at nothing, furious exceedingly when insulted, but as a rule preferring to patrol in shady neighbourhoods, the backwaters of life, where he can peer idly into cracks and holes. See him as he saunters up the path, pretending to be on the look-out for suspicious characters, stopping strangers with impertinent inquiries, leering at that modest wire-worm who is hurrying home. Watch him swaggering to meet a friend whose beat ends at the corner, and with whom he will loiter for the next hour. Suddenly a blossom falls from the orange-tree overhead. His display of energy is now terrific. He dashes about in all directions, jostles the foot-passengers, and then pretends that they had attacked him. He continually loses his own balance, and has to scramble out of worm-holes and dusty crevices; or he comes in collision with a blade of grass which he bravely turns upon and utterly discomfits, and then on a sudden, tail up, he whirls home to report at head-quarters the recent violent volcanic disturbances, which, being at his post, he was fortunately able to suppress! Another and more numerous section of the community of ants are the "loafers," who spend lives of the most laborious idleness. Instead of joining the long thread of honest "worker" ants stretching from the nest to the next garden and busy importing food to the nurseries, they hang about the doors and eke out a day spent in sham industry by retiring at intervals to perform an elaborate toilet. Between whiles the loafer affects a violent energy. He makes a rush along the high road, jostling all the laden returners, stops most of them to ask commonplace questions, or to wonder idly at their burdens, and then, as if struck by a bright idea, or the sudden remembrance of something he had forgotten, he turns sharp round and rushes home—tumbling headlong into the nest with an avalanche of rubbish behind him which it will take the whole colony a long time to bring out again. The loafer, meanwhile, retires to clean his legs. Sometimes also, in order to be thought active and vigilant, he raises a false alarm of danger and skirmishes valiantly in the rear with an imaginary foe, a husk of corn-seed or a thistle down. One such loafer came under my own observation to a miserable end. Thinking to be busy cheaply, he entered into combat with a very small fly. But the small fly was the unsuspected possessor of a powerful sting, whereupon the unhappy loafer, with his tail curled up to his mouth, rolled about in agony, until a "policeman" catching sight of him, and seeing that he was either drunk, riotous, or incapable, nipped him into two pieces, and a "worker" happening to pass by carried him off to the nest as food for the family! An honest ant, on the other hand, has no equal for fixedness of purpose, and an obstinate, unflagging industry. The day breaks, the front door is opened, and the honest ant ascends to daylight. He finds that a passer-by has effaced the track along which he ran so often yesterday, but his memory is good, and natural landmarks abound. He casts about like a pigeon when first thrown up in the air, and then he is off. Straight up the path to the little snag of stone that is sticking out—up one side of it and down the other —over the bank—through a forest of weeds—round a lake of dew, and then, with an extraordinary instinct for a straight line, goes whirling off across the cucumber-bed to some far spot, where he knows is lying a stem of maize heavily laden with grain. Then, with a fraction of a seed in his pincers, he hurries home, hands it over to the commissariat, and is off again for another. And so, if the grain holds out, he will go on until sunset, and when the pluffy, round-faced owls, sitting on the sentinel cypress-trees, are screeching an *ilicet* to the lingering day-birds, the honest ant is busy closing up his doors, and before the mynas passing overhead and calling as they go to belated wanderers have reached the bamboo clumps which sough by the river, he will be sleeping the sleep of the honest. With industry, however, the catalogue of the virtues of ants begins and ends. They have an instinct for hard work, and, useless or not, they do it—in the most laborious way they can; but except for the wisdom which industry argues, ants have no title whatever to the epithet of "wise." Until they learn that to run up one side of a post and down the other is not the quickest way of getting past the post, and that in throwing up mounds on garden-paths they are giving hostages to a ruthless gardener, they can scarcely be accused of even common sense.

THE PARIAH DOG AND THE CAT.

THE gardener holds also in proper detestation the pariah dog and the cat. Why should it be a rule with wandering dogs to philander in the flower-beds, and why should errant cats always dig for treasure where seeds have been lately sown? Why should the former trot about all night amongst the vegetables, or the latter hold their dalliance and serenades in verandahs, their ululations and high falutins at the door of your bed-room? But the pariah dog is a child of sin, and the very prince of paupers, your true licensed loafer, unshackled alike by the regulations of etiquette or the Penal Code, and living beyond the reach of libel. His food is rubbish, and his residence Asia. He carries his bed with him, and pays nothing for carriage. No one stops him for municipal dues. His life is a monotony of sin and ill-usage, and his undertakers are flying overhead. He slouches past, each gesture a major felony, as if, barely escaped from the gallows, he was anticipating suicide, and is for ever running the gauntlet. He is an authority upon misery. This dog, however, is the vagrom species—not the urban pariah that fights in the marketplace for the leg of a meagre hen, or hazards his life on the heel of a shoe; for the municipal cur has grown courageous amongst bare legs, and waxed fat on the memory of the kid's head he whilom stole, treating with contumely and bitter derision the non-municipal dog that lives by following his nose, and dies at a cost of threepence to the State.

Not so the cat. She is a firebrand, and the loadstone of turbulent characters. Although befriended and befed she simulates extreme houselessness, aping the vices without having the excuses of the pariah dog. After eating and drinking at home even to discomfort, she reconnoitres the neighbour's pantry, joins issue with the cat in possession, or skirmishes with the terrier in charge of the verandah. Sudden death she systematically avoids by mysterious evanishments, and after wantonly reappearing at intervals during the evening, settles down for a *soirée musicale* as close to the house as possible—finishing up, as it transpires in the morning, with violent saltations on the latest-made flower-bed.

THE PEA-BOY.

BORN a slave, the pea-boy constitutes himself a tyrant. Unquestioned despot in the garden he drives the scrannel wren and brainless babblers forth from their shelter in the peas, while he fills his own graceless skin with the swelling pulse. Seated by his favourite guava-tree he ruthlessly keeps off marauders, allowing them only to eat their fill elsewhere. He is hired to scare green parrots, but fraternizes with them. The wise crows know him and laugh him to scorn when, between bites, he lifts up his voice to outrage the welkin. Do the little birds care for him? They know him too, and though from courtesy they may yield to his requests to move on, they only wait their time. They know that he will cry three times, once promiscuously, once again as he approaches within sight of the verandah where his employer is sitting, and once again as he dives into the shade of the orange-trees. His mouth is now too full for utterance, and so they straightway hop back merrily they have secreted into their rinds, turning your first gratitude to resentment—fat-skinned and nice to pluck, but hollow-stomached; the modest limes, the fruit of the sick, with their faint colour, fainter flavour and flood of pleasant juice; the splendid shaddock that, weary of ripening, lays itself upon the ground and swells at ease; the rank *popeyas* clustering beneath their coronals of shapely leaves; the pomegranate, with its clustered rubies enflasked in bitter rind; and the melons of many kinds. Nor are these his only prey, for though fruit garnish his meal and furnish dainty trifles to it, he spends the fierce onset of his first hunger on the humbler vegetables. The spare carrot and the solid turnip, the wrinkled lettuce, the tempting tomato with its polished lobes, the celery blanching in its pits, and, hiding their cool stores beneath rough leaves, the prickly cucumbers. Among all these the pea-boy thrives—awhile; for they say pea-boys die young. That is perhaps the reason one never sees pea-men. Or, perhaps, shouting at intervals becomes a second nature to them, and they develope into night-watchmen, and die (for night-watchmen also are short-lived) of bronchial diseases.

THE FROGS.

THE elements had a field-day on Monday last. For many weeks there had been nothing doing —a piping time of heat when the sun and the moon divided the twenty-four hours between them. But all that has been changed, and we had on Monday a parade of all arms. First the wind. But I had heard the jack-tree whispering of what was coming, and among the plantains I saw that there was a secret hatching—and then on a sudden came the strong gust, rain-heralding. The wind came sweeping up, clearing the way for the rain that was close behind, and then the rain, on the earth that was gasping for it, descended in great, round, solemn drops.

And how suddenly did all nature become aware of the change! The grateful earth sent up in quick response its thanks in a scent as fragrant to us in India as is the glorious bouquet of the hay-fields at home. The joyous birds flitted here and there, hymning the bursting of the monsoon, and all the dusty trees broke out into laughing green. The swallow came down from the clouds to hawk among the shrubs, for a strange insect world was abroad, the sudden rain having startled into uncustomary daylight the night-loving moth and the feeble swarm that peoples the crepuscule. The young parrots, insolent though tailless, revelled among the neem-trees' harsh berries, while from the softened earth, in spite of the falling rain, the mynas were busy pulling out the carelessly jocund worms. Even the wretched babblers, who had hoped to raise a second brood of young, and whose nest has in an hour become a dripping pulp, hopped, and not unmirthfully, about. The peacocks came out and danced. Even the crow was festive. But the rain that washed the aloes clean has also soaked out from their lair among them the ringed snakes, so the mungoose is holding high carnival. But hark! Already a frog?—yes, a shrivelled batrachian who, for many sun-plagued weeks had been lying by in a dusty water-pipe, feels suddenly the rush of warm rain-water, and his dusty, shrunken shell is carried out into the aqueduct. With reviving strength he stems the tide, and is soon safely on the bank. Can it be true? and he plunges into the living water again, his shrivelled body—like that curious "Rose of Jericho"—plumping out as it greedily absorbs the grateful liquid, and soon the lean and wretched frog, whom a week ago a hungry crow would have scorned to eat (though a stomach-denying crow is as rare as a Parsee beggar), becomes the same bloated monster in yellow and green that last year harassed us with his importunate demonstrations of pleasure. "And for als moche as" he has thus cheaply attained to respectability, he is inflated with pride. Mandeville thanked God with humility for the keeping of the good company of many lords, but the frog unasked thrusts himself and his amours upon our notice, holding with the Saracens that man is only the younger brother of swine. We welcome the rain, but could do well without the frogs.

"The croaking of frogs," said Martin Luther at his table, "edifies nothing at all; it is mere sophistry and fruitless;" and indeed I wish we were without these vile batrachians. It is not to me at all incredible that the Abderites should have gone into voluntary exile rather than share their country unequally with frogs.

In all "the majesty of mud" they crouch on the weedy bank, croaking proudly to their dames below, who, their speckled bodies concealed, rest their chins upon the puddle-top, croaking in soft reply. Was ever lady wooed with such damp, disheartening circumstance? —the night dark, the sky filled with drifting clouds, a thin rain falling. Round the puddle's sloppy edge—the puddle itself a two-hours' creation—has sprouted up a rank fringe of squashy green-stuff, and in this the moist lover serenades the fair. She would listen flabbily to his beguilements all night long, but suddenly round the corner comes a dog-cart. His position might be heroic, certainly it is ridiculous. Shall he die at his post, be crushed by a whirling wheel for her he loves, or shall he—get out of the way? The earth shakes below the cavalier: this is no time to hesitate: shall he move? *Yes*, and plop! within an inch of his charmer's nose he has landed in the puddle. But such accidents are infrequent: the cavalier, we regret to know, generally serenades all night. By day he sleeps beneath a stone, fitting himself into a dry hole—for frogs dare not go out in the daytime. Crows trifle with them, spit them on their black beaks, and perhaps eat them. Cats, too, will amuse themselves with frogs; even the more chivalrous dog will not disdain to bite a frog when he comes suddenly upon one round a corner. In the evening, however, he takes his hops abroad, makes his meal of ants, and starts off to the nearest place of pleasure. Shall it be the municipal tank, the public assembly-rooms, where the company, though numerous, is very mixed; or some private *soirée musicale*, where the company is select, and the risks of interruption fewer? His journey is not without its peculiar perils. What if, by mistake, he jumps down the well? the one in which live only those two old gentlemen, wretched bachelors, who, sallying forth one night—just such a night as this—to serenade a fair one, mistook their way, saw water glistening, thought they heard her voice, and plumped down twenty feet. They never got out again, and there they are to this day, old and childless; their croak is sullen and defiant, for they are down a deep well, and can't get out. "It *is* enough to sour one's temper," acknowledges our frog, and he goes forth delicately, looking before he leaps. "Living in such a world, I seem to be a frog abiding in a dried-up well"—the Upanishad contains no happier illustration than this.

How the rain pours down! A wall, beneath which he has rested to croak a while, cracks, gapes, and falls. By a miracle and a very long jump he escapes; but his jump has landed him in the lively rivulet which is now swirling down the middle of the road, and so, before he can draw his legs up, or collect his thoughts, he is rolled along with sticks and gravel into a ditch, sucked into a water-pipe, squirted out at the other end, received by a rushing drain, and, ere he can extricate himself, is being whirled along towards the river, where live the barbarous paddy-bird and the ruthless adjutant-crane. Better, he thinks, that the wall had fallen on him. But if he does get safe to his friends, with what gusto is he hailed! At his first note the company becomes aware of a strange presence, and in silence they receive his second; and then they recognize his voice, and with redoubled volume the chorus recommences—for the night.

One of the twenty-one hells of Manu is filled with mud. I believe it to be for the accommodation of frogs.

Part II.

THE INDIAN SEASONS.

1. SUB JOVE FERVIDO.
2. SUB JOVE PLUVIO.
3. SUB JOVE BENIGNO.

1. SUB JOVE FERVIDO.

"And the day shall have a sun
That shall make thee wish it done."

S Manfred speaking of the hot weather, of Mayday in India? The hot weather is palpably here, and the heat of the sun makes the length of the twelve hours intolerable. The mango-bird glances through the groves, and in the early morning announces his beautiful but unwelcome presence with his merle-melody. The koel-cuckoo screams in a crescendo from some deep covert, and the crow-pheasant's note has changed to a sound which must rank among nature's strangest, with the marsh-bittern's weird booming, the drumming of the capercailzie, or the bell-tolling note of the prairie campanile. Now, too, the hornets are hovering round our eaves, and wasps reconnoitre our verandahs. "Of all God's creatures," said Christopher North, "the wasp is the only one eternally out of temper." But he should have said this only of the

British wasp. The *Vespæ* of India, though, from their savage garniture of colours and their ghastly elegance, very formidable to look on, are but feeble folk compared with their banded congener of England, the ruffian in glossy velvet and deep yellow, who assails one at all hours of the summer's day, lurking in fallen fruit, making grocers' shops as dangerous as viper-pits, an empty sugar-keg a very cockatrice den, and spreading dismay at every picnic. But the wasp points this moral— that it requires no brains to annoy. A wasp stings as well without its head as with it.

Flies, too, now assume a prominence to which they are in no way entitled by their merits. Luther hated flies *quia sunt imagines diaboli et hæreticorum*, and with a fine enthusiasm worthy of the great Reformer, he smote Beelzebub in detail. "I am," he said one day, as he sat at his dinner, his Boswell (Lauterbach) taking notes under the table, "I am a great enemy unto flies, for when I have a good book they flock upon it, parade up and down upon it and soil it." So Luther used to kill them with all the malignity of the early Christian. And indeed the fly deserves death. It has no delicacy, and hints are thrown away upon the importunate insect. With a persistent insolence it returns to your nose, perching irreverently upon the feature, until sudden death cuts short its ill-mannered career. In this matter my sympathies are rather with that Roman Emperor who impaled on pins all the flies he could catch, than with

Uncle Toby, who, when he had in his power a ruffianly blue-bottle, let it go out of the window—to fly into his neighbour's house and vex him. The only consolation is that the neighbour probably killed it.

The sun is hardly up yet, so the doors are open. From the garden come the sounds of chattering hot-weather birds. "While eating," said the Shepherd, "say little, but look friendly," but the starlings (to give them their due, and to speak more point-device—the "rose-coloured pastors") do not at all respect the advice of James Hogg, for while eating they say much, looking the while most unfriendly. They have only just arrived from Syria—indeed, in their far-off breeding cliffs, there are still young birds waiting for their wings before leaving for the East—and they lose no time in announcing their arrival. The unhappy owner of the mulberry-grove yonder wages a bitter conflict with them, and from their numbers his pellet-bow thins out many a rosy thief. The red semul-tree is all aflame with burning scarlet, each branch a chandelier lit up with clusters of fiery blossom, and to it in the early heat come flocking, "with tongues all loudness," a motley crowd of birds, thirsting for the cool dew which has been all night collecting in the floral goblets, and been sweetened by the semul's honey. Among them the pastors revel, drinking, fighting, and chattering from early dawn to blazing noon. But as the sun strengthens all nature begins to confess the heat, and even the crow caws sadly. On the water the sun dances with such a blinding sparkle that the panoplied crocodile, apprehensive of asphyxia, will hardly show his scales above the river, and the turtles shut up their telescope necks, shrewdly suspecting a sun-stroke. On the shaded hillside the herded pigs lie dreamily grunting, and in the deep coverts the deer stretch themselves secure. The peasants in the fields have loosed their bullocks for a respite; and while they make their way to the puddles, their masters creep under their grass huts to eat their meal, smoke their pipes, and doze.

But in the cities the heat of noon is worse. There is wanting even the relief of herbage and running water. The white sunlight lies upon the roads so palpable a heat that it might be peeled off: the bare, blinding walls surcharged with heat, refuse to soak in more, and reject upon the air the fervour beating down upon them; in the dusty hollows of the roadside the pariah dogs lie sweltering in dry heat: beneath the trees sit the crows, their beaks agape: the buffaloes are wallowing in the shrunken mud-holes—but not a human being is abroad of his own will. At times a messenger, with his head swathed in cloths, trudges along through the white dust, or a camel, his cloven feet treading the hot, soft surface of the road as if it were again pressing the sand-plains of the Khanates, goes lounging by; but the world holds the midday to be intolerable, and has renounced it, seeking such respite as it may from the terrible breath of that hot wind which is shrivelling up the face of nature, making each tree as dry as the Oak of Mambre, suffocating off it all that has life.

But the punkah-coolie is left outside. His lines have been cast to him on the wrong side of the tattie. The hot wind, whose curses the sweet kiss of the kus-kus turns to blessings, whose oven breath passes into our houses with a borrowed fragrance, finds the punkah-coolie standing undefended in the verandah, and blows upon him; the sun sees him, and as long as he can stares at him; until the punkah-coolie, in the stifling heat of May-day, almost longs for the flooded miseries of Michaelmas. But he has his revenge. In his hands he holds a rope—a punkah-rope—and beneath the punkah sits his master writing. On either side, and all round him piled carefully are arranged papers, light, flimsy sheets, and on each pile lies a paper-weight. And the punkah swings backward and forward with a measured flight, the papers' edges responsive with a rustle to each wave of air. And the writer, wary at first, grows careless. The monotony of the air has put him off his guard, and here and there a paper-weight has been removed. Now is the coolie's time. Sweet is revenge! and suddenly with a jerk the punkah wakes up, sweeping in a wider arc, and with a rustle of many wings the piled papers slide whispering to the floor. But why loiter to enumerate the coolie's small revenges?—the mean tricks by which, when you rise, he flips you in the eye with the punkah fringe, disordering your hair and sweeping it this way and that; the petty retaliation of finding out a hole in the tattie, and flinging water through it on to your matting, angering the dog that was lying in the cool, damp shade. These and such are the coolie's revenges, when the hot weather by which he lives embitters him against his kind. But at night he develops into a fiend, for whom a deep and bitter loathing possesses itself of the hearts of men. It is upon him that the strong man, furious at the sudden cessation of the breeze, makes armed sallies. It is on him that the mosquito-bitten subaltern, wakeful through the oil-lit watches of the night, empties the phial of his wrath and the contents of his wash-hand basin: who shares with the griff's dogs the uncompromising attentions of boot-jacks and riding-whips. For him ingenious youth devises rare traps, cunning pyramids of beer-boxes with a rope attached—curious penalties to make him suffer—for the coolie, after the sun has set, becomes a demoralized machine that requires winding up once every twenty minutes, and is not to be kept going without torture. And thus for eight shillings a month he embitters your life, making the punkah an engine wherewith to oppress you.

It is Cardan I think who advises men to partake sometimes of unwholesome food if they have an extraordinary liking for it; it is not always well, he would tell us, to be of an even virtue. What a poor thing, for instance, were an oyster in constant health: ladies' caskets would then want their pearls. Who does not at times resent the appearance of a friend who is comfortably fat, come weal or woe? The uniform hilarity of Mark Tapley recommends itself to few. But to the punkah-coolie, how inexplicable our theorizing on the evil of monotonous good! To him anything good is so rare, that he at once assimilates it when he meets with it to his ordinary evil. He cannot trust himself to believe the metal in his hand is gold. Given enough he commits a surfeit, and tempted with a little he lusts after too much. Indulgence with the coolie means licence, and a conditional promise a *carte blanche*. And thus he provokes ill-nature. Usually it depends upon the master, whether service be humiliation; but the punkah-coolie is such "a thing of dark imaginings," that he too often defies sympathy.

I have three coolies, and I call them Shadrach, Meshach, and Abednego, for they have stood the test of fire; and Shadrach is an idiot. Upon him the wily Meshach foists his work, and at times even the crass Abednego can shuffle his periods of toil upon the broad shoulders of Shadrach. He is slate-coloured when dry; in the rains he resembles a bheesty's[1] water-skin. In his youth he was neglected, and in his manhood his paunch hath attained an unseemly rotundity. Not that I would have it supposed he is portly. His dimensions have been induced by disease. His thin face knows it, and wears an expression of deprecating humility, to which his conscious legs respond in tremulous emotions. His

[1] The water-carrier.

life is a book without pictures. His existence is set to very sad music. The slightest noise within the house is sufficient to set Shadrach pulling like a bell-ringer on New Year's Eve; but a very few minutes suffice to plunge him into obese oblivion, and then the punkah waggles feebly, until a shout again electrifies it into ferocity. It is always when Shadrach is pulling that the punkah-rope breaks; when more water than usual splashes through the tattie I make sure that the ladle is in Shadrach's hands. Meshach is of another sort. He is the oldest of the three, and when he condescends to the rope, pulls the punkah well. But, as a rule, he allows Shadrach to do his work, for as often as I look out Meshach is lying curled up under a pink cloth asleep, and Shadrach is pulling. He has established a mastery over his fellows, and by virtue, so I believe, of that pink cloth which voluminously girds his wizened frame, exacts a respect to which his claim is forged. They are the Children of the Lotus and he their wise Hermogene. In a grievance Meshach is spokesman, but in the case of a disagreement arising, the master's wrath falls always, somehow, on one of the others. When pay-day comes, Meshach sits familiarly in the verandah with the regular retainers of the household; while Shadrach and Abednego await their wages at a distance standing foolishly, in the sun. Abednego is a man of great physical power, and of something less than average intelligence. He is noisy at times, and may be heard quarrelling with the bheesty who comes to fill the tattie-pots, or grumbling when no one appears to relieve him at the right moment. But altogether he is a harmless animal, turning his hand cheerfully to other work than his own, and even rising to a joke with the gardener. But Meshach holds him in subjection.

But the hot day is passing. The sun is going down the hill, but yet not so fast as to explain the sudden gloom which relieves the sky. In the west has risen a brown cloud, and the far trees tell of a rising wind. It nears swiftly, driving before it a flock of birds. The wind must be high, for the kite cannot keep its balance, and attempts in vain to beat up against it. The crow yields to it without a struggle, and goes drifting eastward; the small birds shoot right and left for shelter. It is a duststorm. The brown cloud has now risen well above the trees, and already the garden is aware of its approach. You can hear the storm gathering up its rustling skirts for a rush through the tree-tops. And on a sudden it sweeps up with a roar, embanked in fine clouds of dust, and strikes the house. At once every door bursts open, or shuts to, the servants shout, the horses in the stables neigh, and while the brief hurricane is passing a pall lies upon the place. Out of windows the sight is limited to a few yards, beyond which may be only mistily made out the forms of strong trees bowing before the fierce blast with their boughs all streaming in one direction. The darkness is like that mysterious murk which rested on the fabled land of Hannyson—"alle covered with darkness withouten any brightnesse or light: so that no man may see ne heren ne no man dar entren in to hem. And natheless thei of the Contree sey that some tyme men heren voys of Folk and Hors nyzenge and Cokkes crowynge. And men witen well that men dwellen there, but knowe not what men." Hark! there *are* voices of folk: from the stables come the "nyzenge of hors;" from the direction of the fowl-house a "voys of cokkes crowynge," and the murk of Hannyson is over all. As suddenly as it came the storm has gone. The verandahs are full of dead leaves, the tattie-door has fallen, and a few tiles are lying on the ground. But the dust-storm has passed on far ahead and is already on the river. Out upon the Ganges the sudden rippling of the water, the brown haze beyond the bank, have warned the native steersman to make for the land. Over his head sweep and circle the anxious river-fowl, the keen-winged terns and piping sand-birds, the egret and the ibis; and as his skiff nears the shore he sees a sudden hurrying on all the large vessel decks, hears the cries of the boatmen as they hasten to haul down the clumsy sails, and in another minute his own boat is rocking about and bumping among the others. The dust-storm travels quickly. Between the banks is sweeping up the sand-laden wind concealing from the huddled boats the temples and the ghat across the river, the bridge that spans it and the sky itself. But only for a minute, for almost before the river has had time to ruffle into waves the storm has passed, and the Ganges is flowing as quietly as ever.

For a while the air is cooler, but the sun has not been blown out, and Parthian-like he shoots his keenest arrows in retreat. And as the shadows lengthen along the ground, the heat changes from that of a bonfire to that of an oven. When the sun is in mid-heaven, we recognize the justice of the heat, abhor it as we may. The sun is hot. But when he has gone, we resent the accursed legacy of stifling heat he leaves us. His posthumous calor is intolerable. It chokes the breath by its dead intensity, like the fell atmosphere that hung round the dragon-daughter of Ypocras in her bedevilled castle in the Isle of Colos.

A wind makes pretence of blowing, but while it borrows heat from the ground, it does not lend it coolness. The city, however, is abroad again. Children go by with their nurses: the shops are doing business. In the bazaars the every-day crowd is noisy, along the roads the red-aproned bheesties sprinkle their feeble handfuls, and the world is out to enjoy such pleasures as it may on May-Day "in the plains." In the country the peasant is brisk again, and trudges away from his work cheerily; bands of women affect to make merry with discordant singing as they pass along the fields; the miry cattle are being herded in the villages. And in the garden the birds assemble to say good-night. They are all in the idlest of humours, and, their day's work over, are sauntering about in the air, and from tree to tree, or congregating in vagrom do-nothing crowds—the elders idle, the younger mischievous. In birddom the crows take the place of gamins, and spend the *mauvais quart d'heure* in vexing their betters. An old kite, tired with his long flights and sulky under the grievance of a shabbily-filled stomach, crouches on the roof, his feathers ruffled about him. He is not looking for food; it is getting too late, and he knows that in half an hour his place will be taken by the owls, and that before long the jackals will be trying to worry a supper off the bones which he scraped for his breakfast. But the crow is in no humour for sentiment. He has stolen during the day, and eaten, enough to make memory a joy for ever. On his full stomach he grows pert, and in his vulgar, street-boy fashion, affronts the ill-fed bird of prey. With a wily step he approaches him from behind, and pulls at his longest tail feather, or sidling alongside pecks at an outstretched wing. Even when inactive, his simple presence worries the kite, for he cannot tell what his tormentor is devising. But he has not long to wait, for the crow, which from a foot off has been derisively studying the kite in silence, suddenly opens his mouth, and utters a cry of warning. The chattering garden is hushed, small birds escape to shelter, the larger fly up into the air, or on to the highest coigns of vantage, and look round for the enemy. The crow, encouraged by success, again warns the world, and his brethren come flocking round, anxious to pester something, but not quite certain as to the danger that threatens. But the crow is equal to the occasion, and by wheeling in a circle round the inoffensive kite, and making a sudden swoop towards it, points out to them the object of his feigned terror. At once his cue is taken, and with a discord of cries, to which Pisani's angry barbiton in the story of *Zanoni* was music, they surround the sulking bird. It seems as if at every swoop they would strike the crouching kite from his perch, but they know too well to tempt the curved beak, the curved talons, and though approaching near they never touch him. The kite has only to make the motion of flight, and his tormentors widen their circles. But he cannot submit to the indignity long, and slowly unfolding his wide wings, the carrion bird launches himself upon the air. Meanwhile the sparrows are clubbing under the roof, and their discussions are noisy. The mynas pace the lawn, exchanging common-places with their fellows by their side, or those who pass homeward overhead. The little birds are slipping into the bushes, where they will pass the hours of sleep; while from everywhere come the voices of nature making arrangements for the night.

One little bird closes the day with a song of thanks. He is a sweet little songster—do you know him?—a dapper bird, dressed, as a gentleman should be in the evening, in black and white, with a shapely figure, a neatly-turned tail, and all the gestures of a bird of the world. Choosing a low bough, one well-leafed, he screens himself from the world, and for an hour pours out upon the hot evening air a low, sweet, throbbing song. He appears to sing unconsciously: his notes run over of their own accord, without any effort. The bird rather thinks aloud in song than sings. I have seen him warbling in the wildest, poorest corner, the knuckle-end, of the garden. At first I thought he was all alone. But soon I saw sitting above him, with every gesture of interested attention, two crested bulbuls, the "nightingales" of Hafiz. They were listening to the little solitary minstrel, recognizing in the pied songster a master of their song. And so he went on singing to his pretty audience until the moon began to rise. And with a sudden rush from behind the citrons' shade the night-jar tumbled out upon the evening air.

2. SUB JOVE PLUVIO.

"For the rain it raineth every day."
Twelfth Night.

IN THE RAINS! Punkah-coolies have had a very narrow escape of making their fortunes, but the vision, if they entertained it, has vanished with the brown grass, has disappeared with the sand-banks in the river, has in fact been washed out by the rains. Punkah-coolies, however, are not the only beings or things affected by this revolution of the seasons, for the despotic monsoon has worked notable changes. The insect world, which during the hot weather was held in such small account, now holds itself supreme. Convinced themselves that entomology is the finest study in the world, the insects carry their doctrine at their tails' point to convince others. Every one must learn and be quite clear about the difference between a black mosquito with grey spots, and a grey mosquito with black spots. There must be no confusion between a fly which stings you if you touch it and a fly which if it touches you stings. No one can pretend to ignore the insect invaders—the bullety beetles and maggoty ants. Nobody can profess to do so. It is impossible to appear unconscious of long-legged terrors that silently drop on your head, or shiny, nodular ones that rush at your face and neck with a buzz in the steamy evenings in the rains. A tarantula on the towel-horse, especially if it is standing on tiptoe, is too palpable, and no one can pretend not to see it there. Spiders weighing an ounce, however harmless, are too big and too puffy to be treated with complete indifference. Then there is a pestilent animal resembling a black-beetle with its head a good deal pulled off, having fish-hooks at the ends of its legs, with which it grips you, and will not let go. Centipedes, enjoying a luxury of legs, (how strange that they are not proud!) think nothing, a mere trifle at most, of leaving all their toes sticking behind them when they run up your legs. It is an undecided point whether the toes do not grow new centipedes; at any rate the centipede grows new toes. Ridiculous round beetles tumble on their backs and scramble and slide about the dinner-table till they get a purchase on the cruet-stand, up which they climb in a deliberate and solemn manner, and having reached the top, go forthwith headlong into the mustard. Sometimes they get out again unperceived, but an irregular track of mustard on the cloth, with a drop wherever the beetle stopped to take breath, leads to the discovery of the wanderer sitting among the salad "and pretending to be a caper." Then again there are oval beetles, which never tumble on their backs, but dart about so quickly that you are uncertain whether something did or did not go into the soup, until you find them at the bottom. Many other insects come to the festive board, unbidden guests; grasshoppers, with great muscular powers, but a deplorable lack of direction; minute money-spiders that drop from your eyebrows by a thread which they make fast to your nose; flimsy-winged flies that are always being singed, and forthwith proceed to spin round on their backs and hum in a high key; straw-coloured crickets that sit and twiddle their long antennæ at you as if they never intended moving again, and then suddenly launch themselves with a jerk into your claret; fat, comfortable-bodied moths with thick, slippery wings, which bang *phut-phut* against the ceiling, until they succeed in dropping themselves down the chimney of the lamp. All these, however, are the ruck, the rabble, the tag-rag and bob-tail that follow the leader—the white ant. The White Ant! What an enormous power this insect wields, and how merciless it is in the exercise of it! Here the houses may not have gardens, there the builder must use no wood. In this place people have to do without carpets, and in that without a public park. Everything must be of metal, glass, or stone, that rests on the ground, even for a few hours, or when you return to it it will be merely the shell of its former self. Ruthless, omnivorous, the white ant respects nothing. And when in the rains it invades the house, what horrors supervene! The lamps are seen through a yellow haze of fluttering things; the side-board is strewn with shed wings; the night-lights sputter in a paste of corpses, and the corners of the rooms are alive with creeping, fluttering ants, less destructive, it is true, than in the "infernal wriggle of maturity," but more noisome because more bulky and more obtrusive. The novelty of wings soon palls upon the white ants—they find they are a snare, and try to get rid of them as soon as possible. They have not forgotten the first few minutes of their winged existence, when they were drifting on the wind with birds all round them, when so many of their brothers and sisters disappeared with a snap of a beak, and when they themselves were only saved from the same fate by being blown into a bush. From this refuge they saw their comrades pouring out of the hole in the mud wall, spreading their weak, wide wings, giving themselves up to the wind, which gave them up to the kites wheeling and re-curving amongst the fluttering swarm, to the crows, noisy and coarse even at their food, to the quick-darting mynas, and the graceful, sliding king-crow. A mongoose on the bank made frequent raids upon the unwinged crowd that clustered at the mouth of the hole, keeping an eye the while on the kites, which ever and anon, with the easiest of curves, but the speed of a crossbow bolt, swooped at him as he vanished into his citadel. Overhead sat a vulture in the sulks, provoked at having been persuaded to come to catch ants ["Give me a good wholesome cat out of the river"], and wondering that the kites could take the trouble to swallow such small morsels. But the vulture is alone in his opinion if he thinks that white ants are not an important feature of the rains. The fields may blush green, and jungles grow, in a week, but unless the white ants and their allies—hard-bodied and soft-bodied—come with the new leaves, the rains would hardly be the rains.

RAINING! and apparently not going to stop. The trees are all standing in their places quiet as whipped children, not a leaf daring to stir while the thunder grumbles and scolds. Now and again comes up a blast of wet wind driving the rain into fine spray before it and shaking all the garden. The bamboos are taken by surprise, and sway in confusion here and there, but, as the wind settles down to blow steadily, their plumed boughs sway in graceful unison. The tough teak-tree hardly condescends to acknowledge the stirring influence, and flaps its thick leaves lazily; the jamun is fluttered from crown to stem; the feathery tamarinds are shivering in consternation, and panic-stricken the acacias toss about their tasselled leaves. There is something almost piteous in the way the plantain receives the rude wind. It throws up its long leaves in an agony, now drops them down again in despair, now flings them helplessly about. But it is not often that there is high wind with the rain. Generally there is only rain—very much. The birds knew what was coming when they saw the drifting clouds being huddled together, and the air has been filled this hour past with their warning cries. They have now gone clamorous home. The green parrots, birds of the world as they are, went over long ago, screaming and streaming by. The crows too, after casting about for a nearer shelter, have flung themselves across the sky towards the hospitable city. But after a long interval come by the last birds, who have dawdled over that "one worm more" too long, calling out as they pass to their comrades far ahead to wait for them; and then, after another while, comes "the very last bird"—for when the storm is at its worst, there is always one more to pass, flying too busily to speak, and scudding heavily across the sloping rain. The young crow meant to have seen the storm out, and so he kept his seat on the roof, and in the insolence of his glossy youth rallied his old relatives escaping from the wet; but a little later, as he flapped his spongy wings ruefully homeward, he regretted that he had not listened to the voice of experience. For the rain is raining—raining as if the water was tired of the world's existence—raining as if the rain hated the earth with its flowers and fruits.

And now the paths begin to show how heavy the fall is. On either side runs down a fussy stream, all pitted with rain-spot dimples, from which the larger stones jut out like pigmy Teneriffes in a mimic Atlantic; but the rain still comes down, and the two fussy streams soon join into a shallow, smoothly-flowing sheet, and there is nothing from bank to bank but water-bubbles hurrying down, yet, haste as they may, they get their crowns broken by the rain-drops before they reach the corner. And now you begin to suspect rain on the sunken lawn; but before long there is no room for mere suspicion, for the level water is showing white through the green grass, in which the shrubs stand ankle-deep. How patiently the flowers wait in their ditches, bending their poor heads to the ground, and turning up their green calices to be pelted! But besides the trees and flowers and washed-out insects, there are but few creatures out in the rain. Here comes a seal carrying a porpoise on his back. No! it is our friend the bheesty.[1] Dripping like a seaweed, a thing of all weathers, he splashes by through the dreary waste of waters like one of the pre-Adamite creatures in the Period of Sludge. Who can want water at such a time as this? you feel inclined to ask, as the shiny bheesty bending under his shiny water-skin squelches past, his red apron, soaked to a deep maroon, clinging to his knees. A servant remembers something left out of doors, and with his master's wrath very present to him, detaches his mouth from the hookah bowl, and with his foolish skirts tucked round his waist, paddles out into the rain, show-

[1] The water-carrier.

ing behind his plaited umbrella like a toadstool on its travels. A young pariah dog goes by less dusty and less miserable than usual. The rain has taken much of the curl out of his tail, but he is, and he knows it, safer in the rain. There are no buggies passing now, from beneath whose hoods, as the vivid lightning leaps out of the black clouds, will leap sharp whip-lashes, curling themselves disagreeably round his thin loins, or tingling across his pink nose. There are no proud carriages with arrogant drivers to be rude to him if he stands still for a minute in the middle of the road to think; no older dogs on the watch to dispute, and probably to ravish from him, his infrequent treasure trove. The worms, too, like the rain, for they can creep easily over the slab ground, opening and shutting up their bodies like telescopes. The dank frogs doat on it. They hop impatiently out, albeit in a stealthy way, from clammy corners behind pillars and under flower-pots, to see if their ditches are filling nicely, and hop back happy. But there is one creature to whom rain is an unmixed abomination—the punkah-coolie, for whom the architect forgot to build a verandah. He sits perched, like a desolate fowl, on an empty beer-box, under a roof of his own construction fearfully and wonderfully made out of remnants of matting; not, however, so cunningly devised but that the resolute, ruthless rain finds its way in, soaking the coolie on his cramped perch, and sopping his wretched "property" in the corner, a brown cloth and a pink cloth, a dingy horse-rug variegated with dingier patches, a shiny brass lota, and a yard of string. But the rain has no bowels.

When it rains there are, to those inside the house, two sounds, a greater and a less, and it is curious, and very characteristic of our humanity, that the less always seems the greater. The one is the great dead sound of falling water—the out-of-doors being rained upon—almost too large to hear. The other is the splashing of our eaves. Outside, the heavens are falling in detail, but the sound comes to us only in its great expanse, more large than loud, heard only as a vast mutter. At our verandah's edge is a poor spout noisily spurting its contents upon the gravel-path, and yet it is only to our own poor spout that we give heed. If it gives a sudden spurt, we say, "How it is raining! just listen"—*to the spout.* The sullen roar of the earth submitting to the rain we hardly remark. We listen to the patch of plantains complaining of every drop that falls upon them, but take no note of the downward rush of water on the long-suffering, silent grass. But when it is raining be so good as to remark the ducks. They are being bred for your table, a private speculation of the cook's, but they are never fed, so they have to feed themselves. Dinner deferred maketh ducks mad, so they sally forth in a quackering series to look for worms. Nevertheless they loiter to wash. Was ever enjoyment more thorough than that of ducks accustomed to live in a cook-house (in the corner

by the stove) who have been let out on a rainy day?
They can hardly waddle for joy, and stagger past jostling
each other with ill-balanced and gawky gestures. And
now they have reached the water. How they bob
their heads and plume their feathers, turning their
beaks over their backs and quackering in subdued
tones! In their element they grow courageous, for the
communist crow who has left his shelter to see "what
on earth those ducks can have got," and who has settled
near them, is promptly charged, beak lowered, by the
drake, who waggles his curly tail in pride as the evil
fowl goes flapping away. But let the ducks quacker
their short lives out in the garden puddles—the carrion
crow is off to the river, for the great river is in flood, and
many a choice morsel, it knows, is floating down to
the sea. Videlicet the succulent kid; guinea-fowls surprised on their nests by the sudden water; young birds
that had sat chirping for help on bush and stone as the
flood rose up and up, the parent birds fluttering round
powerless to help and wild with protracted sorrow;
snakes which hiding in their holes had hoped to tire out
the water, but which, when the banks gave way, were
swept struggling out into the current; the wild cat's
litter, which the poor mother with painful toil had
carried into the deepest cranny of the rock, drowned
in a cluster, and floating down the river to the muggurs.[2]

The muggur is a gross pleb, and his features stamp

[2] Broad-snouted crocodile.

him low-born. His manners are coarse. The wading heifer has hardly time to utter one terror-stricken groan ere she is below the crimsom-bubbled water. Woe to the herdsman if he leads his kine across the ford. The water-fowl floating on the river, the patient ibis, the grave sarus-cranes, fare ill if they tempt the squalid brute. The ghurial[3] is of a finer breed. Living in the water he seeks his food in it, and does not flaunt his Maker with improvidence by wandering on the dry earth in search of sustenance. But at times the coarse admixture of his blood shows out, and he imitates his vulgar cousin in lying by the water's edge, where the grazing kine may loiter, the weary peasant be trudging unobservant towards his home, his little son gathering drift-wood along the flood line as he goes.

And the flood is out over the gardens and fields. Out on the broad lagoon, the grey-white kingfisher, with its shrill cry, is shooting to and fro where yesterday the feeble-winged thrush-babblers were wrangling over worms : the crocodile rests his chin on the grass-knoll where a few hours ago two rats were sporting. See the kingfisher how he darts from his watch-tower, checks suddenly his forward flight, starts upwards for a moment, hovering over the water with craning neck. And now his quick-beating wings close, and straight as a falling aërolite he drops, his keen, strong beak cleaving the way before him. And with what an exultant sweep he

[3] Sharp-snouted crocodile.

comes up, with the fish across his bill! The kingfisher is too proud to blunder: if he touches the water he strikes his prey; but rather than risk failure, he swerves when in his downward course to swerve had seemed impossible, and skimming the ruffled surface goes back to his watch-tower. He would not have his mate on the dead branch yonder see him miss his aim; rather than hazard discomfiture he simulates contempt, turning back with a cheery cry to her side, while the lucky fishlet darts deep among the weeds.

The great river is in flood. "Oh, Indra the Rain-giver, by all thy Vedic glories, we invoke thee, be merciful!" Miles down they will know it by the sudden rush—the bridges of boats that will part asunder, and the clumsy, high-prowed native craft that will sink; but here, where the mischief has its source, where the heavy rain is falling and the deluge brewing, there is nothing to mark the change. But the river swells up secretly, as it were, from underneath. The flood is to be a surprise; and lo, suddenly, the water is spread out on either side, over crops and grass fields. Where are the islands gone on which the wiseacre adjutant-birds were yesterday promenading? Are those babool-trees or fishermen's platforms out yonder in the middle of the river? Surely there used to be a large field hereabouts with a buffalo's whitened skull lying in the corner, and a young mango-tree growing about the middle of it? Can that be the mango-tree yonder where the current takes a sudden swerve? Alas for the squirrels that had their nest in it! Alas for the vagrant guinea-fowl which far from home had hidden her speckly eggs in the tall tussock of sharp-edged grass which grew by the buffalo's skull!

Those two villages yonder were yesterday separated only by a green valley streaked by a hundred footpaths; they now look at each other across a lake. The kine used to know their way home, but are puzzled. Here, they feel certain, is the tree at which yesterday they turned to the right, and this is the path which led them down a hill and up another, but it ends to-day in water! How cautiously they tread their way, sinking lower, lower—so gradually that we can hardly tell that they have begun to swim; but there is now a rod and more between the last cow and the shore where the herdsman stands watching. He sees them climb out on the other side, one behind the other, sees their broad backs sloped against the hill before him. Then they reach the top and lowing break into a trot, disappearing gladly behind the mud walls which contain their food, and the herdsman turns and trudges the circuit of the invading water.

One year the Ganges and the Jumna conspired together to flood the province, and suddenly swelling over their banks, desolated in a night half the busy city of Allahabad. We brought our boat up to the new lagoons, and for a whole day sailed about among nameless islands, great groves of bird-deserted trees, and the ruins of many villages, amid scenes as strange and as beautiful as we shall ever see again. The Máruts, armed with their hundred-jointed bolts and the storm-god, Peru, of the thunder-black hair and beard of lightning-gold, who goes rumbling over the midnight clouds astride a millstone—and all the little hearth-spirits quake at his going and fear falls upon the house—had been abroad for many days. And the river-gods were up at their bidding, and the clouds poured into the rivers, and the rivers drove down to the sea. And before the pitiless rush of the flood, what difference between man and beast? All of them rats alike, poor creeping folk, flooded out of their holes. The same wind and rain tore the crow's nest from the tree and the roof from the native's hut: the same flood carried the two away together. The tiger, the man, and the woodlouse were all on one platform, and that which crept highest was the best among them.

Starting in our boat from the spot where once four cross-roads had met, we crossed over towards the belt of trees that hides the city from sight as you look westward. Deep down beneath us, patient crops of millet were standing in their places, waiting for the water to pass away; acres of broad-leafed melons looked up at our boat as we wound in and out among the trees, and little temples. With some thirty feet of water below us we floated over the brickfields and came to a village, and, skirting the ruins of the suburbs, passed out again through a tope of mango-trees into the open. A garden lay before us. The pillars of the gateway had strange animals upon the tops of them —rampant against shields—but in the flood they looked as if they were standing tiptoe upon their hind legs in the hope of keeping out of the water which lapped over their clawed feet. Over the wall and into the garden. Such a place for Naiads! The tops of plantain-trees instead of lotus pads, for bulrushes bamboo spikes, and instead of water-tangle the fair green crowns of bushes, lit up with blossoms. Rustling through the guava-tops, half-ripened citrons knocking against our boat's keel, we passed out over the other wall of the garden, and found ourselves in a superb canal, avenued on either side with tamarinds, their lowest branches dipping in the flood, and closed in at the further end with a handsome pleasure-house that stood—the only building, except the stone-built temples, that had braved the rush of the escaping river—knee-deep in the water. The scene had all the charms of land and water, without the blemishes of either; for the water had no vulgar banks, no slimy slopes nor leprous sand patches, while the houses had no lower stories, and the round crowns of foliage no unsightly trunks. And there was not a human being in sight! River terns swept in and out the garden trees, furrowing the new water-fields with their orange bills, and resting, when tired, upon the painted balconies of the pleasure-house.

And we rowed past the dwarfed walls with the dreary, pleasant sound of the flood lapping against them, and passed down the stately reach of water till we came to the beautiful temple of Mahadeva, that lifts up its crown of maroon and gold high out of the solemn hush of the trees among which its foundations lie. A golden god glittered at the point — a star to the people. The gate was closed, but as we lay on our oars before it, there came, on the sudden from within, the clanging of the temple bell, that through all the year rings in every hour of night or day! Who was pulling the bell? A merman? Perhaps, forsaken by all his priests, the god himself! We shouted. A tern was startled by the shout, and an owl fell out of a hole in the wall; but there was no reply. Another shout, however, was answered—was it a human voice?— and then we heard the unseen bell-ringer swimming to the gate. It opened after much trouble and splashing, and we floated into the enclosure, "came into the Lake of Silence," our guide swimming alongside. What a strangely sacred place it seemed, this temple to Mahadeva! Up to its terrace in water—the marble bulls couchant in the flood, on which floated here and there the last votive marigolds thrown before the god—the shrine was the very emblem of Faith as it reared its glittering crown skyward up above the creeping, treacherous water—in the hands of the Philistines perhaps, but the Samson nevertheless—its feet in the toils, but head erect to heaven. We all talked in a more or less maudlin way, for sentiment made a fool of each in turn. But no one of us who saw it can forget that strange Indian scene. The gracious water sparkled from wall to wall of the small enclosure, concealing all the dirt of the common earth, and all that was impure or unsightly round the foot of the temple. The flowering bushes rested their blossoms on the water, and the shrubs showed only their green crowns. The squalor and clamour of an Indian temple were all gone, and in their stead was the cleansing, mock-reverent water and the silence of Dreamland. The glamour of the place was strange beyond words. For sound there was only the plash of the water-bird's wing, and the rhythmic lapping of the flood against the balconades. For the view, it was hemmed in by the tree-tops that overlooked the enclosure on all four sides. But within the small area was all that enchantment needed. It was Fairyland, with only a bright summer's sun shining upon everything to remind us of the every-day earth. But suddenly the bell rang again. Fairyland or not, the hours were passing. So we floated out of the doorway again into the exquisite water-road, and sailed away. Look where he would, water, water, water, margined and broken by groves of trees, with here and there a suspicion of ruined houses from which now and again came wailing along the water the cry of some deserted dog. But nothing of every-day life! Where were the villages, with their cracked mud walls? the loitering natives, the roads and their dusty traffic? the creeping, creaking, bullock-carts and the jingling ekkas baboo-laden? There were no parrot-ravaged crops, no muddy buffaloes, no limping, sneaking pariah dogs to remind us of India. Even the kites, sailing in great circles above the broad sunlit water, did not seem the same birds that a few days before wheeled in hopes of offal round the village. The vulture on the palm-top was a very Jatayus among vultures. Where were we then but in Dreamland? A solitary palm—do you remember how Xerxes went out of his way with his army to do homage to the great plane-tree, " that queened it in the desert alone?"—attracted us, and we sailed for it. All great trees grow alone. This one was standing between two round little islands bright with young grass, so close and clean that they looked like green velvet footstools for some giant's use. Their shores were fringed with drift wood and strange jetsam, among which bobbed up and down some great round palm-fruit, and on the top of each island sat a solitary crow. They had come, no doubt, from Kurghalik, the capital (so Thibetan legends say) of crowdom. At any rate, they were Dreamland crows. They were less criminal in appearance than earth crows: they did not insult us by word or gesture, for they did not caw once, nor, when we approached, did they sidle or hop sideways. Some of my readers may not easily believe in such a revolution of crow nature, but those take high ground who maintain that no change of character, however violent, is impossible. Did not

Alcibiades the volupt become a Spartan for the nonce? Remember Saul of Tarsus.

As we landed, one crow raised itself with all the dignity of a better bird, and with three solemn flaps passed over to the central top of the farther island; and when we went there to take possession of it also "in the Queen's name," both of them flapped with three strokes back to the first. And we christened one island Engeddi, for we remembered Holy Writ, "exalted as the palm-tree in Engeddi;" and the other we called the "Loochoo Island," for Loochoo means, in Japanese, "the Islet in a Waste of Waters." (A great deal for a word to mean, but true nevertheless. Humpty-Dumpty would have called it a "portmanteau word.") And we gave the crows commissions as Lieutenant-Governors from Her Majesty Queen Victoria, *quamdiu se bene gesserint*. And then we went on to another island, a long one with a tree in the middle. And under the tree stood a white calf, so we knew at once that this was a water-calf. For there was no land it could have come from within sight, and no human being but ourselves within a mile of it on either side. And at night, when thieves bring their boats to steal what they consider quite an ordinary calf, deserted, they think, by its owner when the swift flood overtook him, the calf no doubt dives under the water, and thus evades them.

The rest of the islands were deserted. The ruins of houses and temples, waist-deep in water, showed that within recent times there had been inhabitants of this strange and beautiful archipelago. Icthyophagi no doubt. There was nothing else for them to eat. But just now the birds were alone. All round us the kingfishers (long may ye live before ye become poor men's barometers!) poised in the air, and wild as the cry of the wild ass in the Bikanir deserts, came to us the scream of the fishing-hawk. But no—the birds were not alone. The flood had driven from the earth its multitude of creeping folk: snakes hung across the forks of trees, or basked on the branches; centipedes crawled upon floating rubbish; and many bushes were black to every tip with thronging ants. In one tree hollow we surprised strange company —a pair of gorgeous dhaman snakes, three bran-new centipedes bright as copper, a most villainous-looking spider, and a gem of a frog, a little metallic creature that showed among the foul crew like the maiden among Comus' companions. We disturbed them rudely, and then went in pursuit of a bandicoot that was swimming to an unwonted roost—poor wretch!—in a citron tree. A little bird was sitting on a bush scratching its head, its day's work over, and thinking of nothing in particular; but a hawk that had had no dinner came by, and gave it something to think about. A pariah dog had a litter upon a patch of tiles, all that remained of a house-roof, and we rescued the starveling brute. A rat floated by in a sieve: another was cruising more drily in a gourd. Look at that squirrel! The imposture is out. So long as he had

the firm earth to fall back upon, he lived bravely enough
in the trees; but now that he has only the trees, he is
starving. The "tree squirrel" forsooth! But was there
no Isis or Osiris, no Apis of the "awful front," nor dog-
headed Anubis, to tell it that the floods were coming?
In Egypt some one tells the crocodiles every year how
high the Nile will rise; for let the sourceless river rise
never so much, the great saurian's eggs are always found
above the reach of the highest wave. But the squirrel
without the ground is better off than a grasshopper without grass to hop in: it is then a poor thing indeed. One
hopped into our boat—a desperate leap for life—such as
egg-seekers take at the dangling rope on St. Kilda's face.
I remember reading in Bacon that "the vigour of the
grasshopper consists only in their voices." That they can
make a noise out of all proportion to their size is true,
but it seems to me that Bacon cast undeservedly a slur
upon the "gaers toop." The particular grasshopper in
point may have been a cripple, but, as a rule, the insect
has a shrewd way of hopping that makes me think
respectfully of its hind legs, and looking into the matter,
I find I am borne out by Sir Thomas Browne, who says,
"whereto (that is leaping) it is very well conformed, for
therein (the grasshopper) the legs behind are longer than
all the body, and make at the second joint acute angles
at a considerable advancement above their bodies." Do
not the French call the grasshopper *sauterelle?* A poor
beetle with the shoulders of Atlas and the thighs of

Hercules, which in drier weather drove headlong through the solid earth, heaving great pebbles up as Enceladus heaves Etna, was sprawling helpless as a moth upon the water. We rescued Goliath and went on. A frog, great with rain water and inordinately puffed up, sat pudgily on a stump. It narrowly escaped with life, for the sight of it enwrathed us. Had the floods, then (a nation's history closing in a sudden stroke of picturesque fate), tragically closed an era, that a spotted frog might go comfortably? The Empire of Assyria expiring with the flames of Sardanapalus' pyre—Babylon poured out under the feet of the Mede with the wine along Belshazzar's palace floor—the Icthyophagi succumbing to the united wrath of a continent's mightiest rivers and gone to feed the fish they fed on! All this that a gape-mouthed batrachian might give itself complacent airs! The earth submerged, the Caucasian a failure, and a frog happy! A deluge whirling men and their houses away to the sea to be a holiday and a Golden Age for a gross amphibian! The idea incensed us, and the frog was in a parlous state. But it escaped.

Meanwhile the sun is setting, and we turn homewards—home in the dusk. The terns are all gone, but in their place the flying-foxes flap heavily along the water, and the owls hail us from all the shadows. How appropriate to the owl are the words of the poet (to the nightingale)—

> "Sweet bird, that shunn'st the noise of folly,
> Most musical, most melancholy."

Sub Jove Pluvio.

The very name too, *ooloo*, is a sweet symphony. The frogs jeered as we passed. One of us recalled the lines—

"You shall have most delightful melodies as soon as you lay to your oars."
"From whom?"
"From swans—the frogs—wondrous ones."

And so through a chorus of exulting batrachians, home again to the solid earth, the noise of men, and the multitudinous chirping of birds.

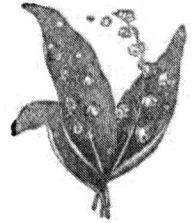

3. SUB JOVE BENIGNO.

> " Ah ! if to thee
> It feels Elysian, how rich to me,
> An exiled mortal, sounds its pleasant name !
> *   *   *   *   *
> O let me cool me zephyr-boughs among ! "
> Endymion.

CHRISTMAS EVE! Overhead is stretched the tent of heaven, and beneath the dome are ranged in full durbar the rajah-planets, attendant on them crowds of courtier-asteroids and stars. The durbar is assembled to welcome Christmas Day. The moon, the Viceroy of the day, presides, and all the feudatory luminaries of the empire are in their places, and the splendour of Hindu rájá or Mahomedan Nawáb is as nothing to that of Orion. How quiet all is! Not a whisper or a movement as the galaxy of night awaits the arrival of Christmas Day.

I was waiting for it too. The night seemed so still and calm, that I felt as if somehow all the rest of the world had stolen away from their homes and gone somewhere, leaving me alone to represent Europe at this reception of Christmas. Not that there were no sounds near me. There was my pony munching gram very audibly, my servants' hookahs sounded more noisily than usual, the dogs under the tree were gnawing bones, and not far from me, crouching beside a fire of wood, three villagers were cleaning a leopard skin. On the jheel behind me the wild geese were settling with congratulatory clamour.

It is curious that those notes which, among birds, give expression to the unamiable feelings of anger and animosity, are more musical than the notes of love and pleasure. Among human beings no passion has evoked such sweet song as love. Among birds, however, the voice of love is more often wanting in sweetness. The bittern, when it calls to its mate, fills the dark reed-beds with the ghostliest sound that man has ever heard from the throat of a bird; the cluck of the wooing cock, that crows so grandly when aroused to wrath or jealousy, is ridiculous; the love-note of the bulbul is an inarticulate animal noise; the crow pheasant—who does not know the *whoo-whoo-whoo* with which this strange bird, hidden in the centre foliage of a tree, summons its brooding mate? The mynas, again, how curious and inappropriate are their love-notes! But show the bulbul another of his sex, and in a voice most musically sweet he challenges the intruder to battle. Look at that strident king-crow swinging on the bamboo's tip. A rival passes, and with a long-drawn whistle he slides through the air, and in melodious antiphony the strangers engage. Let the cock hear the lord of another seraglio emptying his lungs, and with what lusty harmony will he send him back the challenge!

Quite near me, too, the river was flowing over and among large stones, with a constant bubbling and occasional splash. But beyond the few yards lit by my camp fires, in the great, pale, sleeping world lit only by the cold stars, lying far and away beyond my tents, was a monochrome of silence.

And I sat at my tent-door smoking, smoking, thinking of the day I had passed, the days before that, and the days before them. Christmas Eve! In an hour all the bells in England will be ringing in the Day; and, in one home at least, the little ones, an infrequent treat, will be sitting with firelit eyes and cheeks beside the fender, watching the chestnuts roast and the clock creep round to twelve. Yes; at home the children are sitting up, I know, to see Christmas Day in, and waiting, they grow tired. The moment arrives, the hand is at the hour, a chestnut is absorbing all attention, when on a sudden, with a clash from all the steeples, the mad bells fling out their music on the wild night. The great chestnut question is postponed, and, starting from the hearth-rug, the little voices chime together "A Merry Christmas;" and then, with clamorous salutations, the kisses are exchanged, and eager in conversation the little ones climb upstairs to their cosy beds, the bells still clashing out on the keen winter air. And the old folks sit below, and, while the shivering Waits in the street are whining out their hideous thanksgiving, give one more thought to the year that is gone. And the last thought is always a sad one. For after all, on this planet of ours, Life, with its periods of hard work and its intervals of careless leisure, is happy enough. What though we do come into it with our miseries ready-made, and only the materials for our pleasures provided? Somehow I had fashioned my pleasures very much to my liking in the year that was gone, and as I looked back on it, there were few days, cold, hot, or rainy, that did not, now that they were dead, come back to me, as I sat there thinking, as pleasant memories.

Christmas Eve! no bells, no beef, no holly, no mistletoe nearer than the Himalayas! Christmas Eve without a dance, without a single "merry Christmas" wish! Christmas Eve and no chilblains, no miserable Waits, no Christmas boxes or Christmas bills! well, well—the past is the past, a bitter sweet at best; let it pass. Our Christmas Eve in India is a strange affair. Instead of church-bells we have jackals, and instead of holly-berries the weird moon-convolvulus. Look at the ghostly creeper there, holding out its great, dead-white moons of blossom to beautify the owl's day. The natives in the south of India have a legend—the Legend of the Moonflower. There was once, they say, a maiden, exceedingly beautiful, and modest as she was beautiful. To her the admiration of men was a sorrow from morning to night, and her life was made weary with the importunities of her lovers. From her parents she could get no help, for they only said, "Choose one of them for your husband, and you will be left alone by the others." From her friends she got less, for the men called her heartless, and the women said her coyness would be abandoned before a suitor wealthier than her village wooers. But how could they know that one evening, soft and cool, as the maiden sat at her father's porch, and there were no eyes near but the little owls' on the roof and the fireflies' under the tamarinds, there had come out from the guava-trees a stranger youth who had wooed her and won her, and who, with a kiss on her fair, upturned face, had sealed the covenant of their love? But she knew it; and sitting, when the evenings were soft and cool, at her father's porch, she waited for the stranger's return. But he never came back; and her life, sorely vexed by her lovers, became a burden to her, and she prayed for help to the gods. And they, in their pity for her, turned her into the great white moon-plant which, clinging to her father's porch, still waits in the evenings with upturned face for the truant's kiss. For myself, I think they look like saucers. At all events, they are not, according to English tastes, the fit blossom of Christmas time. But then English tastes are not fit for Christmas time in India. The season of frost and ice and snow suggests to us fires, furs, and mulled port-wine; reminds us of skating on ice-covered ponds and dancing in holly-bright rooms. The Christmas bills are a skeleton to some; but even with the butcher, the baker, and the grocer dancing a cannibalic war-dance at the area-gate, there is hardly a home where Christmas is not "merry," and Hans Andersen's sexton, who struck the boy for laughing on Christmas Eve, is considered a prodigy of infamy. But "the cold weather," as we in India are pleased to call the months at the end and beginning of the year does not suggest mirthfulness to our Aryan brother: it shrivels him up. Months ago, when the sun was killing the northern blood within us, the lizards lay happily basking on the hot stones, the coppery Danais flitted at ease about the shrubs above which the air of mid-day stood shimmering and tremulous with heat, and our Aryan brothers, stretched in the shade of tree and wall, were content with God's earth. But now that the crisp morning air lends vigour to English limbs, making home intolerable and a wild out-door life a necessity, the lizard has shrunk into a crack of the wall, the Danais is hybernating, and our Aryan brother creeps about his daily avocations with the desiccated appearance of a frozen frog, or sits in dormouse torpidity with his knees about his ears. The revenge of the Briton is delicious to him, and in the cold weather he triumphs over the Aryan brother who in May and June was rustling comfortably in gauze and muslin. The morning ride or walk when the air is keen is to him (*pace* Charles Lamb) as a passage of the Red Sea, every native an Egyptian, and he laughs, like King Olaf at the thin beggar, to see the wretched Hindu, robbing his spare legs to protect his head, pass by silent with the misery of cold. At night he finds them curled into inconceivable spaces under their blankets—and such blankets! a network of rough strings with hairs stretching across the interstices, the very ghosts of blankets at which Witney would hold its woolly sides with laughter. And with many-folded cloths round his benumbed head, over all the blanket, the Hindu walks deaf under your horse's nose, stands before your buggy-wheels like a frost-bitten paddy-bird. The Tamils call the paddy-bird "the blind idiot." On a December morning the pompous chuprassie has no more self-respect than a sparrow or a hill sheep,[1] and a child may play with a constable as men handle a hybernating cobra. The fat bunyas are no more seen lolling beneath their shameeanas; the Hindu, in short, is "occultated."

In the shop yonder where earthen vessels are sold—a shilling would buy the whole stock-in-trade—with the walls festooned with chalky-surfaced chillums, the floor

---

[1] A flock of hill sheep will meet at a corner of the zigzag path a burdened pony and the leader of them will turn aside. Soon the woolly tribe are in headlong flight down the steep hill side, and the tattoo, astonished at his own importance, passes on in sole possession of the scanty way.

piled high with clay pots, sits the owner frozen and voluminously swathed. He is not proud of his shop: there is none of the assumption of the thriving merchant about him. He is too cold to concern himself about his wares, for when his neighbours want pots they will, he knows, come to him; if they do not want pots, advertisements and invitations are thrown away. Shouting is a mere waste of carbon. So he spends his mornings perched on the edge of his threshold, polishing his chattering teeth with a stick, and rinsing his mouth from the brass lotah beside him. In the next house there are no wares to sell, but in the centre, on a rag of carpet, sits a puffy man painting, with much facial contortions, and frequent applications of his numbed fingers to the charcoal burning near him, the face of a mud monkey-god. By his side are ranged rows of similar monkey-gods awaiting their turn of the brush that shall tip their heads with scarlet and their tails with yellow. Before the door sits a careful mother scouring her daughter's head with mud. Here two shivering baboos shiny with patent leather as to their feet, with oil as to their heads, and with many folds of a gaudy comforter about their necks, are climbing cautiously into an ekka, a pariah dog half awake watching the operation with a dubious wagging of its tail. One and all are extinguished, suppressed, occultated, by the cold.

Christmas Day! Can this be really Yule-tide?

> "December came with mirth men needs must make
> E'en for the empty days and leisure's sake."

So opens the Prologue of a modern poet's story of how, in those olden days when dolphins knew good music when they heard it, and love it was that made the world go round—the Strong Man came down to the Tyrian merchant-vessel swinging in Mycenæ Bay, and taking the helm himself when the great east wind began to blow its fiercest, steered straight for the island where the daughters of old Hesperus the Wise guarded the tree with the golden fruit. It is a December poem, and yet the scene of it is laid in a land where the boughs were blossomed and " unknown flowers bent down before their feet "—where there were the lilies of spring in the grass, the fruit of autumn on the trees, and, over all, the warm light of a summer sun. Well for the poet that his song was of olden times! The reader is content in his December tale to take him at his word, to see wade off from the shingle the man

> " Who had a lion's skin cast over him
> So wrought with gold that the fell show'd but dim
> Betwixt the threads."

And afterwards to see him at the foot of the golden-fruited tree, in the land of roses and singing-birds, standing where

> " Three damsels stood naked from head to feet,
> Save for the glory of their hair."

We see him pick the red-gleaming apples, note the branch spring back, and then watch him, with the round fruit in his hand, go down across the lawn dappled with flowers and fallen fruit to the Tyrian ship again.

"His name is Hercules,
And e'en ye Asian folk have heard of him."

We "Asian folk" have indeed heard of a land where, by some pantomime of nature, roses are winter flowers and fruit ripen in December, where there are singing-birds instead of only cock-robins and turkeys, and where the damsels of the land instead of nestling in chinchilla or sable's fur stand about in a rural manner, much as did the Hesperids. We know too that in that land there was once a magic tree with golden pagoda coin for fruit, which strong men, coming across the sea in ships of trade, shook at will. But vegetables are not auriferous now. The "Golden Pippin" is a species of apple unhappily extinct, and *Sir Epicure Mammon* was not far from the mark when he lumped "Jason's fleece, Jove's shower, and the Hesperian garden" as "all abstract riddles of the philosopher's stone."

But though the tree is gone, the country is much what it was in the Genesis of Anglo-India—the antediluvian period that preceded the Mutiny of 1857. It is still a land of juggling seasons. December comes round as usual, and with it Christmas Day and its marigolds, and men, having no work to do,—

> "Mirth needs must make
> E'en for the empty days and leisure's sake."

I have spent Christmas in England, and there was honest merriment enough. And on the doorstep without, birds and beggars alike shared in the sudden flow of Christmas goodwill.

I have also spent Christmas Day in India, but not all the marigolds of Cathay will firk up Christmas spirits, or make me throw crumbs to a blue jay. The blue jay would not eat them in the first place, for there are plenty of flying things abroad for him to eat. But even if that unpleasant bird, with its very un-Christmas plumage of sunny blue, were to turn frugivorous for the nonce to humour me since "Christmas comes but once a year," I would not feed him. I have no Yule-tide humour about me for there is no Christmas around me. The jests of nature are too long in the telling to be mirthful. The crops have been yellow with mustard blossom this week past, the gardens in all their glory for many weeks, and how all of a sudden, and simply because it is the 25th of December, can I feel more at peace with all men than I did last Thursday? If Nature would only meet me half way, or even the robins of the country wear red waistcoats instead of red seats to their trousers, I would try and squeeze some seasonable festivity into my thoughts. But it is out of the question. Why! there is at this moment a punkah-puller outside the tent talking about the affairs of the hot weather, and dunning my servant for four annas to which he prefers a forged claim. He was always interesting that cooly. They are a feeble folk, the most of them—the coneys amongst mankind—and the intelligent are in a desperate minority. Look round at the crowds of coolies whose life is a long yarn of grey toil, crossed at intervals with tawdry threads of lazy, worthless self-indulgence. Of " remembrance fallen from heaven " they have none. When the high gods sat down to fashion them, they must—to turn the poet's words—have wrought with more weeping than laughter, more loathing than love. Swinburne has said that they gave them also "life"—enough, perhaps, to make the bitterness of humanity keen to them; and that they gave them "light"—enough to illustrate the deadliness of all life's pleasures, and to show them the way to their graves. They have limbs and a shadow, and yet I doubt if poor Peter Schlemil would have exchanged his bedevilled existence for theirs. The flight of time they congratulate themselves upon, and nobility of deed or speech in a finer race does not affect the level of their minds, for they cannot even think splendidly.

But this particular cooly of mine was an interesting study, for he owned a cow. How he got it I cannot guess, for he did not look like a person with rich relatives to remember him in a will, and with his own money he could not have bought it. Nor could he have stolen it, for his legal ownership was ostentatiously displayed at all hours. Yet it was not a cow to be very proud of. It was not a big cow, and gave no milk. Nor did it drag anything about it—a cart or vehicle of any kind. But it was very cheerful. It played bo-peep with my terrier between the pillars of the porch, and from pure light-heartedness used to scour about the compound with its tail, from an ecstasy of mirthfulness, curled up into a knot on its back. It trotted about a good deal in the mornings, and when its owner was not pulling my punkah, he was generally running about slowly and indefinitely after it. The cow always went much faster than the cooly, for I never saw him catch it except when it was standing still, and when he came up with it he never seemed to know what he should do next. He used to pull it about in a possessive manner, and jerk its rope as if he wished it to move—first in the direction of the compound-gate, and the cow would cheerfully trot alongside of him, but on a sudden there would be a violent jerk, and the cow would find the cooly pulling in the opposite direction, whither it would, without demur, follow him. Whatever the change of programme, the cow acquiesced in it with the utmost heartiness; and thus, after having blithely proceeded a little in each direction, it generally found itself pretty much where it started from. The cooly would then carefully tether his property to the largest weed that was near, the cow looking on at the elaborate process with a contemplative aspect; after which, the cooly having

Sub Jove Benigno.

turned to go, it would eat the weed up, and gaily accompany its master towards the verandah. The cow was quite useless to the cooly, and he could not demonstrate his ownership by doing anything with it. So he would sometimes throw stones at it—just to show that the cow was his. It was all pride, the pride of ownership; and though the cow cost him at least threepence a week, for it was regularly impounded for frolicsome trespass, he never parted with it. But I was obliged to part with the cooly, for one day the wind being high—the Scythians said wind was the principle of life—the cow was unusually lively, and, after a preliminary canter round the garden with the terrier, it proceeded, in spite of the gardener, to execute a fantastic but violent *pas seul* upon a croquet ground which was in course of construction. I felt, therefore, compelled to ask the cooly to take his cow away and not to bring it back again. Nor did he, for he never came back himself—not, at any rate, until the punkahs had been put away in the lumber-room, and the tatties were gone, wherever old tatties go. His cow, I think, must be dead now, for he seems to have nothing to do but to loaf about with my camp, waiting for me to pay him the four annas of wages which he tries to prove is due to him.

* * * * *

Now, what a strange thing human nature is! Here I have been protesting for the last hour that I had no Christmas foolery left in me; and yet I have this moment paid that punkah cooly the four annas he has no claim to—and which on principle, as I have told my wife every day for the last month, I have refused for two months to pay him—*just because it was Christmas Day!* To increase the absurdity, I had to confess the reason to him! For having sworn solemnly on all the rules of arithmetic that I did not owe him one farthing, I was obliged to give a decent explanation for my sudden acknowledgment of the debt; and how could I, before my servants, better maintain my dignity, and at the same time get rid of an importunate cooly, than by making him a present of his extortionate demand in full, because it was a "Feast day with us Christians."

For yet another Christmas, then, have I kept alive a Yule spark!

I look up at the poem lying open before me, and with a fateful response that may compare with the unhappy King's *Virgilii Sortes*, the book replies—

"Cast no least thing thou lovedst once away,
  Since yet perchance thine eyes shall see the day."

Perchance, indeed, we *shall* all see another Christmas Day "at home," and among romping children and welcoming friends rekindle the smouldering Yule spark lit at an honest English Christmas blaze.

much w
carefully t
near, the co
a contemplati

Part III.

AMONG THE CROPS.

AMONG THE CROPS.
THE SPARROW.
THE WOLF.
THE JACKALS.
SUDHOO.
BUGGOO, THE CHOWKEYDAR.
THE GNOME OF THE HILLOCK.
THE BHEESTY'S MOTHER.
THE FAQUIR.
THE GARDEN OF KHUSRU.
THE SYCE'S CHILDREN.
MOSQUITOES.

AMONG THE CROPS.

IT is noteworthy that when in India we praise the beauties of English landscape we, perhaps unconsciously, keep close to our mind's eye the commoner and less picturesque types. The memory when recalling England goes back with complacency to the simpler charms of cottage and corn-field, river and meadow, park and woodland. Few can remember easily any misty, pine-clad mountains, broad levels of green fen or purple heather, or cliffs where the pied sea-birds cluster; but it costs none of us an effort to remember the scenery of half our shires—the undulating grass-land, broken only by hedgerows, farms, and copses; the green lanes and brooks; here a stretch of corn-field, there a patch of preserve, and dotted over the whole, trees, white cottage walls, and church spires. A clear sunlight —bright but not hot—lies upon the land, whitening the sheep on the slope, the shirts of the reapers in the fields, the cattle beneath the pollard willows which mark the course of the flowing brook. These little things are the real charms of English scenery. We boast (to use language of the "Bird o-freedom Soarin" type) no frantic rivers bursting through granite gorges and plunging themselves in mist and thunder into black abysses, no eternal snows with almighty eagles, no oceans of savannah flecked with bison herds. We have mossy banks and beds of primroses, instead of glaciers and cataracts, beech-tree avenues and squirrels, instead of volcanoes and anacondas. Perhaps we are envious; and yet for myself I am satisfied to boast of the cosy, happy scenery of England as if it were very beautiful, and many besides myself really believe it to be so. We confess to finding much that is very grateful in full corn-fields, and a real charm, though of a quiet and placid kind, in a reach of meadow-land.

The beauty of crops is not chiefly one of colour: its appeal to the eye is largely through the mind, and therefrom perhaps more pleasing; but this is only of our English crops. The crops of India are very beautiful in themselves. The dark, close-growing pulses, with their yellow, broom-like blossom; the tall, broad-leaved millet crops which in a month shoot up from a pallid vernal green to autumnal yellows, browns, and scarlets; the sugar-cane and the handsome castor-oil plant, the gaudy safflower, the arums and the flax, the fields of cucumbers and melons starred with great yellow blossoms, vary the rustic scenery, and are themselves beautiful. Their appearance, the artistic contrast of colour, the strange foliage, strike us as we pass. And yet when we leave the country we shall remember not the corn-fields or pastures, the village or suburban scenery, but the Himalayas or the Nilgherries, great rivers, great rocks, and great jungle gorges. We shall seldom recall the broad fields of cotton, luxuriant tobacco, or white-flowered poppy; the gram fields whence the clamorous jackals sweep at nightfall, the tall jowar with the raised platforms in the midst whereon the small-voiced native squatting tries to scare the lusty parrots; the bujra which the sparrows love, and of which, with all the brutality of a majority, they possess themselves.

THE SPARROW.

SEE them now. The lean-limbed watchman may clatter his bird-scare, may lift up his voice in remonstrance from dewy morn to dewy eve, but he will not turn the multitudinous sparrow from the evil tenor of his way. It is Emile Souvestre who calls the sparrow "the nightingale of the roofs," and says that "our chimney-pots are his forests, and our slates his grass-plots," but I incline to take a less lenient view of the genus *Passer* than does the kindly essayist. As we resent the likeness to ourselves which the monkey tribes possess, so we feel injured by the familiar communism of the sparrow. He professes, though in another arc, to move on the same plane with man—our chimney-pots are his chimney-pots, and our slates his slates, but our forests and grass-plots are none the less his also. There is, in his deportment, none of the deference of a stranger when he crosses your threshold—the conscious humility of an interloper. His entry is that of a conqueror into a hostile city, or of a king into another's palace. He begins by putting himself on an equality with you, but soon arrogates superiority. He holds that man by natural selection will develope into the sparrow, but in his present hybrid stage criticizes him as the fool who builds houses for the wise (sparrow) to live in. Show me a man's house, and I will show you a sparrow's castle; point out, if you can, a stable which the sparrow does not share with the horses. *Vos non vobis nidificatis* he chirps, and points the quotation by hopping with dirty feet across your verandah. He is the gamin of birds—chief vagabond of the air. He it is who mocks the illustrious stranger, jay or owl, crowds without payment into places of public amusement, disturbs Divine service by a fracas with his kind on the altar rails, or, irreverent fowl! perches above the Ten Commandments and chirps monotonously through the sermon. His cranial development is very poor—flat atop, showing a deplorable lack of respect; bulgy behind, typical of gross amativeness and gluttony; and puffy at the sides, where lodge the devils of destructiveness, evil-speaking, lying, and slandering. This Bohemian communist has broken through—worn out—the resentment of man; we no longer resist his intrusions or retaliate for his rapine. He has acquired a prescriptive right to be iniquitous and go unpunished. But he does not understand this. In his conceit he insolently imagines that he has compelled acquiescence and treats us as a conquered race. He takes alms by force, making charity a military requisition; and, to quote Aurifaber's preface to one of Luther's works, "his gorged paunch is puffed up with uncivil pride." In another world he will be met with strolling in the Valley of Jehoshaphat, flower in hand—the badge of one who has benefited his fellow-man—will swagger through the fields of amaranth and moly, and take to himself more than his share of asphodel.

THE WOLF.

S the sparrow possesses himself of the corn-fields by day, so do the jackals and the wolf by night. In all their excursions these brigands start from the cover of some high standing crop, returning to them when morning endangers, or when sudden alarm prompts to precipitate flight. Here now may be lurking the were-wolf, the Ishmael of the pack, who while its kindred are swinging at a gallop (so leisurely it seems, but leaving the horse and his rider far behind) across the dark-shadowed ravines and through the black crops that lie like clouds upon the moonlit country, here pulling down a bewildered antelope, there flashing upon some feeble sheepfold and carrying off, slung across its strong back, a speckled kid or yearling lamb—who, while its kin are fighting round some carcase in the distant jungle, boldly visits the abodes of man himself, roams in his public places and along his roads, loiters in his pleasure-grounds, passes like a lost shadow across his croquet lawn, haunts his verandahs, perhaps even steals into his carpeted rooms.

A nurse lies sleeping on the floor, her charge asleep in her arms. The wolf listens. He can hear slumbrous voices mumbling beneath the porch, can hear the guttural hookah answering to the long-drawn breath of the smoker, can smell the sick scent of the tobacco. The wolf, his grey coat hardly showing against the matting, lies down beside the sleeping pair and pauses. A house-dog far away is answering defiantly the maniac jackals sweeping past him in full cry. Then the wolf bends his furred head, and with his thick, warm tongue licks the baby out of its nurse's arms. The poor woman feels the gentle warmth, unconsciously presses the baby closer for a moment, but her grasp begins to relax. The moist, soft touch of the wild beast's tongue, its bated breath, melt her fingers open. One by one they loosen their guardian hold, the wrists sink apart, and gently from her bosom the baby slides back against the soft coat of the crouching wolf. It does not wake: the wolf rises. The house is still; drowsy voices are still mumbling. The house-dog has lain down self-satisfied, for the jackals have passed by. The baby is lying on the ground. Again the furred head, the eyes sparkling, is bent down. There is one sudden snap, and the cruel teeth have closed in the baby's throat. A feeble cry, and the nurse springs up to hear the rustle of swift feet across the matting, to feel her own foot slip in the blood at her side. The terrible truth flashes upon her, and at her cry the house is up. But the wolf and the baby are gone. The house-dog wonders if that was really something which passed between him and the garden wall—thinks not—growls angrily, and turns to sleep. But ask the owl sitting on the vinery what it sees, that it turns its head over its back. Ask the wheeling bats. They will tell you that a wolf has just passed beneath them carrying across its back a little child, and that it has leaped the aloe hedge and is gone into that black grain crop beyond. The mother may weep, the servants chatter, and the father search, but the baby is gone. The wolf is with it, lying again by its side, but its touch is now rough and cruel, its breath is short-drawn and fierce, for the wolf is hungry and the children of men are dainty food.

Next harvest a little skull will perhaps be found in the corner of the field under that bush, if the jackals have not already rolled it back to its father's door.

THE JACKALS.

THE jackal is the bug, the green parrot, among mammals. He has a use, I presume, for everything, they say, was created for a purpose, but it is not an easy one to guess. Musk-rats were made, I know, to eat cock-roaches, and very well they understand their *raison d'être;* spiders for the suppression of blue-bottles; mosquitoes for (in their larva state) the purification of standing water, and, in their winged state, to teach man humility and to give an impulse to the manufacture of bed-curtains. These are all evident, but why were jackals created? To eat refuse. Then what is the use of the vulture, the kite, the pariah dog, and the multitude of necrophagous beetles? That jackals do not eat much refuse, or much anything, is evident from their chronic famine. Catch a jackal at any time, and he is hungry. Open his criminal stomach, and what are its contents?—the better part of a young curry-fowl and a pair of kid gloves. Now neither of these were "refuse." His own bowels witness against him. The deceased found the chicken shut out by accident from the hen-house, and the kid-gloves he picked up at a door in the verandah. It is evident that jackals were not created for the purposes of scavengering, for though they certainly do, when occasion offers, spend a jovial night over a carcase, the carrion birds would have done the job as well, as quickly, and more quietly, when morning broke, so that at best the jackal is a superfluity, an appendix, a supplement. But he does not admit this. He arrogates to himself a definite mission on earth, and would have himself recognized a complete ego. And he succeeds so far, in that he renders it impossible for us to ignore his existence. Nobody is afraid of him except Sweet Seventeen and the cat; but everybody loathes him. With a crash of sudden sound the pack shatter the crystal silence of the summer's night, shivering with their demoniac clamour the starlit stillness into pieces, each throat a fiend's, each fiend double-throated.

I confess to a lofty dislike of the jackal, but he has a grim and dirty humour which sits well upon him. He is always the first to tell us of his presence, bursting out pleasantly in an explosion of discord from, it seems, under the chair on which we are dozing through our night-cap pipe—just when we were moralizing, maudlin, over Nature "hushed in fond repose," or listening, sentimental, as the "trailing garments of the Night sweep through her marble halls." We had almost forgotten

India, quite forgotten the jackal, when it loosed upon us that swarm of noises. A jackal, I take it, has a wider gamut than any beast, bird, fowl, fish, or instrument since Paganini's fiddle. Let the Howling Monkey brag of his *os hyoides*, and fright his native forests with his awful utterances, or the mocking-bird mimic in a breath the voice of all creation, the jackal is their master. With one simple tongue—no *os hyoides*, no powers of mimicry—he will let you have, from his own proper throat, such a variety of hideous sounds, that were he long-winded you should curse your gods. But our burdens are meted out to us according to the width of our backs, and quick-tongued humanity has been spared this crime of blasphemy by the short wind given to jackals. Not that they cannot run for leagues, or be worried by dogs till they are as limp as sodden leather and afterwards revive, but they cannot long use both legs and tongue together. Hear them now, as they pass in full cry through that urhur crop. The first crash, as of brass bands bedevilled, is over; one brute tries to rekindle the foul riot, but only gets up a duet, his breath fails—the solo lasts a minute longer—a few snaps, howls, groans, and yells, and the corn-field is as silent as ever: the jackal pack has swept by. These ghastly jesters have another jibe, one which they never tire of playing off. It is to roll bones into your presence. Stuck fast in the muddy bed of a distant nullah is the skeleton of a sheep. Times are hard, watch-dogs are on the alert, and the jackals revisit the well-picked bones. The skull is dragged out, mumbled across half a field, fought over for another hundred yards, and in the end pleasantly deposited at your bathroom door.

SUDHOO.

THERE, beneath the two jujube-trees, in the corner of the field, stands Sudhoo's cottage. Its walls are not so strong as those the beaver builds, nor so high as the ant-hills of Peru, but it is nevertheless the abode of man, and of a man who has a story to his life. Before the door stands the architect and owner, Sudhoo the stalwart, and this is his story.

One day there came by, on an ambling pony, a many-folded blanket for a saddle, a fat and bare-limbed money-lender, who stopped before the cottage door and called out for his money. "I have none," said the stalwart Sudhoo, "but my cow will calve next week." The rich man turned his creased back towards the mud-walled cottage, and went off between the high green walls of the dal crop, threatening with much perspiration and blasphemy the peasant with the law. And Sudhoo wondered for a moment whether it could be the will of his gods that he should be insulted thus, and his mind was soon made up. His gods could not wish it—was not his cow going to calve soon? So he strode after the fat money-lender. But before he went he took from its place, where it leant against the wall, the long bamboo which, when a lad, he had cut from before the house. The clump was then a bush, and this the longest shoot upon it; but now an ample tope waved high above his cottage. Then he tightened his waistband, and strode after the fat money-lender. Between the green walls of the dal crop he came up with him. "Wait for your money till my cow calves!" he cried. The other sneered, and shook his head, and then—thwack! across the creasy back came the long bamboo. "There's your interest! Go to the court, and say it was I who paid you," said Sudhoo, with a great laugh, to the man of money, as he lay roaring among the dal, and he strode back to his cottage. His pipe was filled, and he sat beneath the jujube-trees, staring across the corn-fields to where, in the far distance, shone white the walls of the Englishman's court-house, whence at nightfall he would hear Buggoo the watchman shouting, and whence evil for him would come he knew on the morrow, and he smoked on and wondered that his gods should wish him evil. And the evil came, and the peasant was sent to prison. But before he went he turned to his wife: "Wife of Sudhoo, water the melon-patch till I come back, and take care of the cow. See that Buggoo does not steal the milk."

A river and many long miles of corn-land. much brick

and mortar, lay between him and his mud-walled cottage beneath the jujube-trees. But his heart was there, and in the early morning he thought of his wife, alone, pulling up water from the deep well, and he watched the thin stream trickling across the dry ground, and then he remembered—his cow. Was the calf born? Would that Buggoo steal the milk? And in the evening he remembered his pleasant hookah, his wife cooking his spiced meal, and the clear moonlight; and as he thought of them he waxed very angry, and said to himself, "I will go and see if the calf is born." So he rose, struck his feeble fetters against the stone bench, with the larger fragment forced back the bolt of his door, strode out into the prison-yard, felled the knock-kneed warder, climbed the wall, and before the warder had picked up his turban, was running like a quail through the close-growing stems of the high crops—here cowering along the edge of a garden, there leaping a watercourse. But straight as the evening bee hive-ward went Sudhoo home.

The moon is shining, two little owls are chuckling consumedly as he passes to his house, a woman's voice is humming a long tune on one note, when suddenly the stalwart peasant strides out from the black shade of the grain crop. The owls tumble away into the night air with a horrified cluck, the humming ceases, and a man's voice says, "Wife of Sudhoo, has the cow calved?" "No," she said, "it may to-morrow." And his pipe was filled and he smoked on till his wife was asleep. Then he rose, drew the water from the well till he had filled all the trenches,—" She will have little work to-morrow,"—and as the day was breaking he ate his meal, and with his blanket went out into the dal field, stretched out his great limbs, and was fast asleep, while the officers of the law came to his house and sought him. And so time passed : while he smoked, his wife sang to him, and while she slept he worked, through the day lying hid in the thick dal crop. At last the cow calved, and Sudhoo saw the little stranger into the world, and a few nights afterwards he and his wife went off between those green walls which had seen the money-lender smitten from his thin-legged tattoo, and sold the cow and calf; and while he sent his wife with the money to pay the fat money-lender, he went himself back to the prison beyond the river. He climbed back over the wall, spoke kindly to the knock-kneed warder who would have fled from him, strode through the prison-yard, and sate him down in his cell. " Tell the jailer that Sudhoo has come back." " Why," asked the Englishman, " did you break away ? and why, after you had escaped so well, did you come back ?" Then made answer the stalwart Sudhoo : " I went to be with my cow while she calved, and now that the calf is born I have come back."

BUGGOO, THE CHOWKEYDAR.[1]

ND who was Buggoo? Buggoo was a chowkeydar, and Sudhoo's neighbour. That wigwam is Buggoo's house ; his wants are very few. Besides, he seldom sees his house by daylight—the crank walls and the latticed roof look well enough by night; so Buggoo is contented with his house, and as he sallies forth to his work, he sings a hideous refrain at the pitch of his voice, answering cheerily the owls. The chowkeydar is an animal *sui generis*, and the one only species of his genus. The family has but a single order —chowkeydars—and besides them there is no other, neither any varieties. His childhood is a tradition. Perhaps in early youth he was a pea-boy, and so acquired a taste for grotesque shouting; but it is more reasonable to suppose that he never was a boy. He was born adult. He exists by night, and his days are divided into moonlight and pitchy darkness. For one-

[1] The night-watchman.

half his life he has no shadow. He knows of the sun, but is not intimate with it; the constellations he is familiar with, taking his time from the rise and decline of the Hesperids or Orion. For the periods of his working hours Nature has provided him a chronometer. If when he comes to his work the bats are still fluttering in and out the rafters, he says, "I am up betimes, 'tis early;" the Great Bear is aslope, and he says, "The day's work is half over;" and when the jackal cries the third time at the break of dawn he says, "I feel sleepy, night approaches." And in this he cuts himself off from his kind, sets himself apart from humanity, in that at early morn he goes yawning home like the beasts of the forest and not forth to his work like the sons of men. He knows what the sun is like—to see a festival he has sat up the live-long day. More than this Buggoo does not know. Bats are his sparrows and moths his flies: an afternoon is as secret from him as the Feast of Fatima or the system of computation by quaternions, and of the sun at mid-day he speaks as we speak of the Southern Cross. He holds it his duty to sleep all day, because he has been up all night, though he sleeps all night to shirk his duty. Now and again he wakes up and clears his throat to let the world know it, or yells in answer to some distant friend; but he does little more. When he comes first he seizes his iron-shod club of office, and striking it as he goes against the dull ground makes the circuit of the house. Beneath the porch he loiters with the servant who is sitting up to see his master home—saunters round the corner, and as he passes each bed-room door startles the night with an unearthly cry, putting the jackals to shame, or breaks off suddenly in the middle to choke in a reassuring manner. He then coughs defiantly, hiccups, and passes on—tramp! tramp! "And Beauty sate in the hall waiting for him, and at last she heard him coming, tramp! tramp! striking his club upon the ground, and suddenly round the corner came—the Beast." The chowkeydar meanwhile has reached his blanket stretched out in a sheltered place, has scared away the cat which had taken possession of it, and is asleep.

THE GNOME OF THE HILLOCK;
OR,
HATCHET-HEADS OF THE COPPER AGE.

BUGGOO'S daughter is married to Madhoo, the second cousin of the nephew of the other Madhoo, whose sister-in-law was the wife of the villager Anúp—the Anúp who, as the following village legend tells us, was killed by the Gnome of the Hillock.

Beside the hillock, round which when young he had often played, upon which in the infantine mimicry of piety he had years before built him a little obelisk to the god Mahadeo, and over which in a fine cloud of tempered green the old tamarind planted by an ancestor hung its boughs, the villager Anúp was ploughing up the tough ground. He had for half his lifetime been fighting a mysterious law-suit which his grandfather had begun, and which,—his adversaries through three generations having died out, and the papers relating to it having all been destroyed in the memorable year of the Pindaris' raid,—he had won at last. Perhaps the curly-headed English youth who had come to the village to decide the case, bringing with him a little dog,—harmless-looking, bow-legged, and of a whitish colour, but which during the half-hour it stayed in the village had found time to kill Anúp's great pariah cur,—knew little about the matter. Perhaps Anúp was in the right. At all events, there he was in that hot May day driving his plough through the long-disputed patch of ground. When the sun was straight above him, and his shadow had fallen about his feet, Anúp bethought him of his midday pulse, his tobacco and siesta; so he unyoked his languid oxen, turned his plough upside down, and went towards the tamarind-tree.

Ha! why does he turn his head to the hillock? What does he see? There is something glittering on the hillock's side. In a moment the old man is kneeling at the hillock, and with a sharp stone digging out the metal. Can it be *gold?* Gold it surely is! some pounds of it, and beaten into a hatchet shape. Could the stories of his village then be true? Was this hillock in truth the dwelling-place of the gnome Jubandwip? Was it a huge dumpling of jewels with just a paste of turf? Anúp thought no longer of sleeping, but sat down, trying to settle in his fat village mind how he should craftily outwit the Gnome of the Hillock. He sat wondering and looking at the lump of metal in his hand, until the sun went down, and his oxen, bewildered at the unwonted holiday that had been thrust upon them, began to think of their evening measure of chaff, and turning towards Anúp's village, browsed their way homeward. But Anúp was not thinking of his supper or of his oxen. He had grown rich—was the usurer of his village: lent out money at high interest to his fellows: had bought half a district in a year of dearth; rode about in a comfortable palanquin; his name was "Babu Anúpjee," and his house flowed with ghee and buttermilk. So he sat dreaming. But where was the money wherewith to do this—the wand to transform the scene? True, he had a handsome lump in his hand, but this was not sufficient to build all the castles he had planned, to buy the estate, and to flood his house with buttermilk and ghee. Where was the rest? *In the hillock there, ten yards from him.*

And as he looked at it, he almost thought he saw the luminous gold burning in a yellow shimmer through the cracks of the grey mould and between the roots of the brown turf, and Anúp could bear waiting no longer. So he ran to the hillock, and with his hands began pulling down the protruding lumps, and either hand, where it touched the hillock, rested on a chill surface, and with either hand he drew out a lump of gold. Was he bewitched? Wherever he put his hand, gold came up to meet the palm, and he had only to close his fingers to draw out the rich wedges. But soon the weight of his treasure warned Anúp that it he would not have his secret known, he must hide what he had already got and return for more on the morrow. Hark! a cry—the light of lanterns—"Anúp! Anúp!" The villagers had seen the bullocks come home alone, and thinking that a tiger had carried off their master, his heirs were coming out to find him. "Anúp! Anúp!" The villager got up, twisted two or three lumps into his waist-cloth, and shouting in reply was soon the centre of a circle of sympathetic friends. "He had fallen asleep: his oxen had gone off: the cries of his good friends had awakened him: he thanked them; he was quite well, a little rheumatic perhaps; there was no tiger in the case." And so he got home with his secret kept, and when the evening meal was over—his fellows wondered that he refused to join the social hubble-bubble—he went into his dark hovel and fingered his gold. And as he caressed it, he remembered with fear the other wedges lying uncared for at the hillock's foot. After long thinking he crept out of his village. The whole country was asleep, except where, half a mile off, a fire was fitfully gleaming. The voice of the night-watchman indulging in a harmless song came towards him, broken only by the yelping of village curs and the clamour of the wild geese passing a mile overhead. There was no moon as Anúp stole along. What a start those jackals gave him! Were the ill-omened beasts of carrion calling to him to go back! Tumbling through the air above him came an owl, surely warning him from the hillock. A great bat wheeled round his head! But Anúp stumbled along and reached the hillock at last. From the tamarind-tree above him rustled out some night-fowl, and Anúp, his hair bristling on his head, listened to its wild cry till it died away in the dark distance, before he felt the courage in him to approach the gnome's thesauron. And just as he had made up his mind to go up to the hillock, and had moved out from beneath the tamarind-tree, he felt the earth tremble beneath him. And lo! the hillock burst open, and from the gleaming rent poured out a stream of molten gold. And from the rippling metal sprang a royal tiger, a noble beast with red-hot eyes, great claws and fangs of flame, and his whole skin lambent with a phosphorous lustre, on which, like the scars of old burns, showed out his hundred stripes. And on the tiger's back sat the outraged Gnome of the Hillock, the very terrible Jubandwip!

And Anúp knew him. A thousand legends told of his coal-black face, white eyes, and teeth as long and large as a man's arm, of his dank red hair and his feet that grasped like hands. It was indeed the Gnome of the Hillock, and he spoke in a voice like an elephant's trumpeting: "You have disturbed me from my rest; you have robbed me of my gold." Then there was silence. Only the tiger's deep breathing, the pulses of the throbbing earth, and the hissing of the hot gold. Then Anúp, trembling, offered to go home and bring the fatal treasure back, to leave that village for ever, and to tell the gnome's secret to no man. "Was not the gnome his god, and he poor Anúp, a ploughman?" But Jubandwip would have none of the dross; and cried out, "You may keep the gold: four hairs from your knee is the price I ask." But Anúp would not sell himself to the devil, and refused.

Again the gnome thundered out his words, and again Anúp whispered a faint refusal. And lo! on a sudden the molten gold was rolled back like a carpet upon itself, enfolded the tiger and its terrible rider, and, crumpling up, was gathered again into the hillock, whose two sides closed with a tremendous sound that shook the ground again. But in the midst of the great sound Anúp heard clearly the word "BEWARE!" and all the wakened hill-sides heard it, and shouted it to each other again and again, until in the distance the sound died away—"BEWARE—BE—WARE—WARE."

Next day Anúp was found lying in his hovel nearly dead, and for many days it was thought he could not live. And when he woke up to life he was blind and deaf. What was life to him? He would go back to the hillock and sell himself to Jubandwip. Better be rich and well, the slave of a devil, than a blind pauper. So he asked his fellows to yoke his plough for him and take him to the patch of ground by the hillock near the tamarind-tree. So they took him, and standing apart saw the blind man guiding his plough hither and thither. The bullocks, fat with no work, pulled to one side and the other; but the poor villager could not guide them, and the children among the by-standers laughed at the old man ploughing in a circle, and lashing the empty air with his stick. And on a sudden, while all were watching the zigzag furrows, the plough grazed the hillock, and with an angry snap broke off short! The bullocks, released from their weight, scampered hither and thither. A tuft of green herbage hung from the hillock side, and they stretched up their yoked necks to crop it. Those watching saw the weed pulled down towards their mouths, when suddenly the beasts together fell forward, their foreheads resting on the hillock. Anúp, feeling with his hands, came up to them. But what use a goad to drive on dead bullocks? Then Anúp put out his hand to the hillock, and below his fingers he felt the chill touch of gold, and as if he had touched a serpent he sprang back —"Jubandwip! Jubandwip!" The villagers standing round heard the shout, and screaming "Jubandwip! Jubandwip!" fled to the village, leaving the old cripple by his bullocks. And the day wore on. The villagers crept back in twos and threes, and from a distance watched him. He was praying to the gnome, but they could not hear his words. He was kneeling and taking something from his knee. And then they saw him rise, and, as if he had his eyes, he walked, unconscious of their presence, muttering through their midst as they shrunk back to give him way, straight to his own hovel. At the door he paused, calling to his little nephew, "Tota! Tota!" and an urchin came running to him.

The old man took the child's hand, and led him back the villagers, who had crowded round, making way for the couple and following in a whispering, frightened pack at his heels—old people and young; men forgetting their work, women their face-cloths, children their play. And Anúp reached his field—the bullocks like grey marble figures knelt before the hillock, their foreheads resting against the turf, the broken plough lay by them—and neared the awful mound. The curious villagers, pressing from behind, stood closer, and they heard the blind Anúp invoke the gnome: "*Jubandwip! lord, I pay the price: I have brought him;*"—and the little child, sobbing with fear, was lifted with one hand by the old man, while with the other he felt the air before him towards the hillock. All the villagers stood round horror-stricken, open-eyed, open-mouthed, silent as a company of the dead. Anúp had reached the hillock, and raising the child with both hands he placed it on the top. There was a little scream—and then the child lay quiet.

The vultures were gathering in the sky. Already round the hillock and the kneeling kine swooped the carrion kites. Anúp was rubbing his eyes, putting his fingers in his ears. Did he see the dead child? Could he hear the scream of the carrion kites? No; for the gnome was mocking him, and he cried out "Jubandwip! lord, I have paid the price: thou hast him, and yet I am blind. Jubandwip, my lord, oh Jubandwip! I am still blind—blind." But there came no answer, and all the villagers, horror-stricken and sick, turned away, creeping homeward one behind the other. One who turned to look at the cripple by the hillock saw that round him were sweeping and hovering a cloud of hungry birds, while ever and again came the piteous cry across the fields, "I am still blind, oh Jubandwip! my lord, I am still blind!"

And some hours after, as the evening was greying, the young men of the village, with the daring of ignorance in them, crept towards the field, and climbing up the bank, parted the tussocks of sword-grass that grew like a mane along it, and peered through at the hillock. But where are the bullocks—the child—the old man? Ask that jackal dragging something under the tamarind-tree. No need to ask.

Months after the Government officers came to the village to learn the truth. And the young curly-headed Englishman, with his dog behind him, went into Anúp's hovel—no one had dared to enter it—and in it he found some wedges of metal. "Hatchet-heads," he called them, "of the Copper Age."

THE BHEESTY'S MOTHER.

SCOTUS has formally damned Solomon. How then shall any one be found to speak well of the bheesty's[1] mother? And in truth the appearance of the dame forbids much courtesy in her biographer; her wrinkles are more than a breach of good manners; they are an affront to the commonwealth. She is lean, lean as the cannibal kine in Pharaoh's vision, altogether an osseous process, and her angles scorn while they defy concealment. She looks as old as Alexander's elephant, as haggard as a Sybil or the San-Po, and might stand for the eldritch beldame who, Buddhists say, rows the spirits of the dead across the River Sandza. If, as it is said, the poor are the world's feet, then is the bheesty's mother a toe-nail—a corn upon a small toe, for she has positively sounded the nadir depths of poverty. She lives, as birds die, out of sight, but dies with great cir-

[1] The water-carrier.

cumstance. The bheesty will make holiday at her demise, and amid the ululations of the green-skirted clan, her old husk will be put to bed for its long sleep.

Watch her where she sits at the door of that poor hut in which she lives, herself the poorest guest. Is she thinking? Are the frogs who croak in the well beside her thinking? "There is no gown," said Luther, "that worse becomes a woman than that she should appear to be wise"—then is the bheesty's mother becomingly clothed, for it is impossible to discern in her any semblance of wisdom. For her, indeed, there is hardly a world at all. Around her are the neems rank with clustered berries, the tamarind flushed with its strange, beautiful bloom, the aloe uprearing from a rose of spiked leaves its bell-hung shafts,—all the beauties of an Indian garden; but the bheesty's mother does not think of them. The amaltas-tree may wag its yellow bunches at her or make itself ridiculous with sausage pods; but what does the bheesty's mother care for change of seasons? She hears the lusty koel-cuckoo, the bold, black Mephistopheles of birddom that brings troubles into many a married bird's nest, scream the hot months through. But she has forgotten the legends of her youth, and listens to it screaming infamy to its mottled-plumaged mate without a thought. But still she has not forgotten all her youth; for as you pass her, her withered old hands rise instinctively to her head, to veil her face from a stranger's gaze. Pitiful old woman! Perhaps memory is a painful effort to you. To the very old retrospect often is an ungrateful process. The past is rough with broken expectations, sharp-gravelled with splintered hopes, and Memory has tender feet.

THE FAQUIR.

ONE of the specialities of India which on my first landing amused me greatly was the Faquir; and my amusement has not even now staled into indifference towards him. Indeed, to me, who am in no way put to discomfort by them, the faquirs seem entitled to receive from us some of that respect which in spendthrift ignorance the natives so lavishly spend on them. Not like chrysalis inviting reverence by the proud splendour of his robes, but by the humility of nakedness commanding it, the faquir holds in awe the starveling poor. His old rags are his regalia, his filth an ermine more honoured than the bee-sprent mantle of the Napoleons. Cleaving to his ancient staff, as Luther clung to his tattered psalter, the faquir stakes his fortunes upon the poverty of his appointments. And in a country where gorgeousness of apparal marks out the wearer as one to whom honour is due, the mean trappings of the man of God appeal forcibly to the popular superstition. His tithes are collected without dispute; his cheques upon Heaven discounted on earth without murmuring. Clearing for himself a spot by a frequented road, he seats himself, and by the very grimness of his presence compels respect from the passers-by, who, the ignorant of them, invest him with all the traditional glories of the great ascetics of story, and from their own scanty store give in alms to the old man whose age and helpless misery they can see, and whose virtue they cannot disprove. To the robuster temperament of Europeans the mumping hypocrisies of faquirs, their ostentatious display of wretchedness and deformity, their cruel power over the very poor, are causes for regret; but the natives take high ground when they assert their right to believe in the ultimate harvest to be reaped from charities sown at random along the roads of life. To us it all seems degrading, and we wonder at them much as we would have wondered at the strange people of Menantra who worshipped the Southern Cross, and paid with their shell-currency for slabs of blue sleep. Yet in a useless way it is pleasant to pretend to admire credulity, for superstitions were the earliest outcome of reason, the *primitiæ*, the first products of a simple humanity cursed by the absence of history, aching for a Past and for something to believe in. Being thus prompted by only natural and beautiful aspirations, they cannot be altogether unworthy of admiration. When the Chinese hold up, for the example of youth, the fabled glories of

Yu the Great, or the virtuous splendour of the mother of Shangte, we respect the motive; and if the faquir, openly professing to be in his own person an exemplar of the self-denying recluses of old, a concrete expression of the abstract virtue of self-denial, holds himself out to public notice as a living warning against the vanities of life, should we altogether protest against him? It is well to be reminded that Heaven is not only for the successful—well even for the wretched peasant who has neither love for the Past nor pleasure in the Present, to have some hope in the Future. And if he believes the hideous mendicant when he says that he has the powers of a St. Patrick or St. Christopher; that the calf he brings with him tricked out with cowries, possesses within its silly head the rain-compelling Yedh; and in that belief gives him a handful of dry grains, let him, in God's name, give it. He is, after all, not much worse in doing so, than those who, innocent of all superstition, recognize bodily misery and do not relieve it.

It was a faquir, the dirtiest of his kind, that led me to discover that there was poetry of a sort in cutting one's throat. He was a laboriously dirty man for where others of the brigade had only a layer of dust upon their heads, he had a little mound: the unkempt locks of his comrades were on him replaced by ropes, matted with horrid cosmetics into the hair and hanging down to his knees. His body was grey as a squirrel's tail with a pigment of dust laid on with some viscous matter: the ribs on either side stood out staring from the daubing of ochre laid in the hollows between each. Small in size, and of unparalleled leanness, this incarnation of dirt had attracted my attention. It was the day of a great fair held at the junction of two holy rivers, and I was purchasing some curiosities at a stall, haggling over cornelian marbles, agate beads, and absurd alabaster monkey-gods and goddesses with very rounded limbs and silly faces, when this faquir came sauntering up. While I was watching him he lifted a little Mahadeo off the stall, and from his own head reverentially transferred a wafer of Ganges mud to the occiput of the idol. Then leisurely turning round, he picked his way through the holy-water bottles exposed for sale upon the sand, as carefully as the superstitious Chinaman picks his way across a floor that is strewn with papers, and approached the Sacred Rivers. Heedless of the worshippers who, all up and down, a mile's length on either hand, fringed the river; heedless of the thousand bathers, of the shameless clamour of the Brahmans and of the invocations of the crowd, the suicide stepped composedly into the water, and with even steps advanced until his long rope-matted hair was trailing in the mingling rivers. And then on a sudden a knife flashed from the waistcloth. A wild cry—that rose above all the clamour of the fair, startled the myriads into a moment of silence, and turned all eyes towards him—went up to "GUNGAGEE." There was just one rapid, desperate motion of the arm, and the next moment under the rippling water lay the body of the faquir. And his soul had gone to its gods. The cry was of course "the fanatical screech of a bigoted idolator about to sacrifice himself to some vile heathen deity," but nevertheless there rang through it a very human cry of ordinary pain. Perhaps the faquir was doing what he thought his duty at the bitter price of life. Perhaps this earth of ours had attractions even for such as him, and that serving a less bloody god he might have preferred to live.

THE GARDEN OF KHUSRU.

"MAN is a noble animal, splendid in ashes and pompous in the grave, solemnizing nativities and deaths with equal lustre, nor omitting ceremonies of bravery in the infimy of his nature." Three tombs, grand witnesses, in an age of credulous sceptics, of an old world splendid even in its graves, stand together; and men have forgotten in whose honour they were built. The piled masonry keeps its secret, though in the still night they must surely talk of the barbaric and magnificent Past. And well for us that they speak in cypher. Round them was once spread a kingly garden, royal in size and royal in its wealth of foliage. In ranged order the black-shaded mango-trees lined each broad road and met overhead, and under them, as in cathedral cloisters, wandered long ago the worshippers of the great of old—"the dead but sceptred sovereigns who still rule our spirits from their urns." In remote corners were massed dark thickets of close-blossomed, heavy-fruited ·itrons. Robust shrubs of jessamine and oleander relieved in large colours the levels of green turf which were spread between. For the garden was a garden only for the ghosts of the great dead and for the reverent living, and in its appointments was stately. And now? Prim beds lie flat upon the ground, central in each a single blossomed rose—a miracle it may be of its species —while on painted supports cling cobwebs of faint exotic flowers. Small plants, with the demeanour of the well-educated stand at even distances from one another, each keeping itself to its own hole. A round pond makes two ducks indifferently happy; the squirrels exult in a new vinery stocked with choice grapes, and many a gardener grows mysteriously fat on the products of an English vegetable garden. A well-metalled road sweeps round between croquet lawns, to a band-stand made out of pickings from one of the old tombs. The same great wall, bearded with a century's growth of creepers, and tanned with a hundred years of sun, still belts the garden; but over and beyond it, the high tombs can now see slim, smooth-faced walls, red and white, the puny offspring of haste and economy, that after a single cycle of the seasons will succumb to the forces of Nature.

And once there stood before the tombs a triad of great trees, giants of their kind and very beautiful. For in the whole world there is surely not a tree more beautiful than a tamarind of old growth. But early one warm summer's morning the grandest of the three came down. The massive limbs it had thrown out were more than its bole could bear, and with a great cry, like that of the stricken Titan in the poem of Endymion, the splendid vegetable fell. Came down from out the sky that grand dome of feathery green that for two centuries had grandly shaded the mausoleum of a king. What a poem might not be written on its fall! The long strange history it had survived—the whole story of England in India,—and then that morning when it fell. The old tree, bearing up bravely through the still hours under the terrible secret that, as the night wore on, became known to every, the smallest, spray upon its branches; the sympathizing night which set each trembling leaf with a tear-drop of dew; the moon coming up late and sadly with a dark cloud across her face; the wistful low-voiced wind which breathed so tenderly, for the last time caressing the foliage. "Go by, go by," spoke the tree to the sad-voiced wind, "to my brother by the Eastern Tomb, and tell him that when the sun rises to-morrow, it will shine triumphant across from space to space. I shall not be here then to hold up my deep breast against him, take all his heat, and beat off for half the day his rays from the ground behind me. For two centuries, and day after day"—and then the sudden death-shudder shot from crown to root. A momentary quiver, and lo! with a great groan the cleft trunk reeled asunder, and for a mile round they knew the old tree had fallen.

Years ago the tombs stood deep-planted in the religious grove, their presence only guessed at by the flights of pigeons wheeling round their minarets; but to-day they are a landmark for miles round, performing the vulgarest function of a church steeple. The same parrots nestle in the fretwork of their parapets; the flying foxes still hang beneath the eaves: from their highest peaks the craning kites scan the country round, just as they did a century ago; and the villain sparrow, as of old in Tobit's wall, defiles the crevices with his last year's nests. But beneath how changed the scene, how changed the forms that people it! When Neill's avenging guns roared his illicet to the presumptuous Moulvi,[1] and his followers crushed through the embattled gates in terror-stricken flight, the old tombs said good-bye to the Past. Since then they have welcomed to their shade no cavalcades like those of the Persian kings, no gaudy camps like that of the Mahomedan rebel. How strange their present, how exquisitely profane! The shelter of the grim mausoleum is used for a fancy bazaar, and Christians dance to music upon the threshold of the Moslems' tombs.

[1] The rebel Moulvi, Liakat Ali, held his camp in the Khusru Bagh (the Garden of Khusru) at Allahabad during the Mutiny.

THE SYCE'S CHILDREN

A BUNGALOW is no sooner tenanted than the compound belonging to it is occupied by the vanguard of a hireling army. By-and-by the main body of domestics takes possession, and for a month afterwards camp-followers keep dropping in. They trickle, percolate, into your premises. They steal in after nightfall or while you are at dinner, and without your knowledge their household gods strike a firm root. Legislation is no preventive, for, forbid what you like, the camp-followers will come. All that mysterious chain of relatives known as "*bhai*"[1] have to find a dwelling-place, and find it they will. But the evil does not end here. Each man seems to bring a wife and two mothers with him, and these bring their sisters' children, until at last, coming home suddenly it may be, or paying without warning an unwonted visit to your stables, you are surprised

[1] The family circle, which, with natives, may be expanded at pleasure so as to embrace an extraordinary number of individuals.

to find a baby-warren flourishing on your estate. These are "the syce's[1] children." Of course they cannot all be, but somehow, ask whom you will, the answer is the same, "Those, your lordship, are the syce's children." It doesn't matter that nine of them are all the same age, that there are no two alike in features, that your syce is only eighteen years of age—"Those, your lordship, are the syce's children." Well, God help thee, syce! Thy income is five thin rupees per mensem, and thy reputed progeny worthy of Solomon in his best days. The syce's children! They are the Philistines—the Amalekites in our borders. They are as the sand of the sea, but much browner. Images of their Maker, cast in mud and never baked. Made of dust, they live in it, and cost their parents nothing for playthings. They all seem of one sex, but which it were difficult to remember: their shaven heads suggest nothing. In habits they are social and inoffensive, but their appearance is a crime. Their bodies bulge, and their skins are full of creases. In the hot weather they go "sky-clad," and in the cold they are not much otherwise. And yet there is about the syce's children, about all native children, a touch of nature which appeals to our common kinship. When met with in by-places these morsels, these half-anna bits of humanity, rise from the ground on which, sitting, they were unperceived, to make a salutation to the passing stranger: and search the round world over, there is nothing more beau-

---

[1] Groom.

tiful than the reverence of the Eastern when made by little children. Their small fat bodies double softly up, and the tiny hands rise from the dusty road slowly to the forehead, while the large eyes, divided between the gravity of the occasion and the curiosity of the child, look up shyly through the dark fingers.

Their fatness is not, however, the result of a healthy assimilation of food—the natural increment of a body fed upon nutritive juices. It is rather the smooth inflation of a puff-ball or a mushroom-stalk—a rotundity induced by air and water. Like some puppies they swell out upon little food, and starving assume the deportment of comfortable circumstances. Troubles, however, except those of a hungry stomach, seem never to approach them. They are ignorant of the sorrows of the children of the West, where the minor is subjected to much unnatural barbarity in his cradle years.

And here I would digress for a short space, in order that I may acquaint the reader that it is my opinion that the hardiness and vigour, both of mind and body, which have made Britons such as they are, are owing not, as some writers, both of ancient and modern times, would have us believe, to the harshness and extremes of the Northern climate; nor yet, as other authors opine, to any mongrel admixture of Teuton and Celtic blood in us; but solely to the ordeal of ill-treatment and bodily suffering to which as babies we are all put. The Apache Indians will leave their offspring on the first night after their birth in the open air, to see whether they be worthy to live, and the Spartans of old were wont to dip their new born babies into icy water for the same purpose. Thus, too, do the nurses of England compress our stomachs with interminable bandages to the expulsion of our breath, in order that our long-windedness may be put to a severe proof, and the curriculum of physics and unsavoury waters, through which the baby attains to childhood, are ordained to try our digestions and to temper our internal economy to harsh influences. But to return to the syce's children.

Troubles, as I have said, seem to keep far from them, for their handling is left all to Nature, who fends all evils save those of her own making from them. Their mouths are always ready to open to show the laughing sparkling teeth: the black-berry eyes, when fear is absent, are always mirthful. Their amusements are, however, very few. The stock-in-trade of the Western waif—oyster-shells and a dead cat—are not available. Oysters there are not, and once dead nothing belongs to man in India. It is the fee of the carrion kites who have been waiting for it since its birth. They play, therefore, with themselves and with the surface of the ground. These playthings are always with them, and they seem to need no more. Nor, as may readily be understood, does this sport incite to much hilarity. The syce's children are generally of a solemn kind. They may be seen, or glimpses of them, threading their slow silent way through a gram field, one behind the other, like pigmy Hurons on a war trail. There is no laughter at the pigeons tumbling overhead, no jostling to pick up a fallen feather, no clapping of hands when they startle out a jackal or see a cat. They do not catch the butterflies, pick the flowers, or quarrel with each other. Their playground reached, they sit down and discuss the dust. They pile it into little graves and funereally deck it with religious marigolds. But they do not dance round it. They survey it pleased, but quiet. Perhaps, as they have seen their fathers do, they crouch to it and whisper the names of gods, but more often they sit round it, and add to or take from their structure, as the long pondered thought induces them, and then, when the sinking sun reminds them of their evening meal, they rise up and in single file pass on home again. But it must not be supposed they are unhappy, for they are evidently quite happy. Only they use it sadly. The Brahminism of the country has infected them, and they take their pleasure passively—as well they may. They live on equal terms with the pariah dogs—the jackals are one grade below, their father's master's horses one grade above them. They exist, as it were, only two feet from the ground, arch-images of wasted and creeping humanity. They are quite harmless, for there is not even any mischief for them to do. Glass to break there is none, and stone-throwing does not find favour with them. They steal fruit, it is true, but only such as grows half wild in remote corners of the garden

—berries which the green parrots and squirrels share unequally with them. No one loses by their criminal misappropriations, for no one but they would eat them. Poor little fragments, I could speak of you longer but—I say it kindly—you are not worth it.

MOSQUITOES.

IT seems hard to believe that there should be any confusion as to the identity of mosquitoes, and equally hard to believe that any one should pretend ignorance. Yet an English traveller, affecting moreover to be a "naturalist" lately said that Indian mosquitoes, *our* mosquitoes, are only small sandflies, and speaks of "a terrible pest, the sancudos," as the real mosquito. If, at the time of writing, the author had a few of these "small sandflies" reconnoitring the back of his head, he was justified in writing anything; but he should have said so, or else he stands the risk of being sent by public subscription to Phocis, to undergo a course of hellebore—a reputed cure for lunacy; or back to India, that he might be tormented out of his flippancy. For flippancy it is, of the gravest criminal order, to speak of these tragical enormities—these sinful abominations that badger us out of our judgment and leave us viciously wretched—as "small sandflies." Small they may be in appearance, but they are Behemoths and colossal in crime. It was "the little foxes" that ate Isaiah's grapes, and "the little people" who killed "the very strong man Kwasind" on the river Taquamènaw. But *sandflies* they are not. Sandflies are quite a distinct evil—as different from mosquitoes as prussic acid is from arsenic, or the Plague of Boils and Blains from the Black Death.

Not that naturalists look at them æsthetically or morally; they understand them only in their quiddity and head-thorax-and-tail physicalities. They call a mosquito by a difficult name, and know how its stomach looks under a microscope; but this view, though intrinsically valuable, scarcely rises to the subject. There is no feeling, no poetry in such treatment of a mosquito, and the knowledge is of a lower kind than seems required. The desiderata of information are, whether it is possible that mosquitoes lead very unhappy lives, and scream at you only under pressure of great domestic affliction, and whether they couldn't be subjected to utilization, made into glue or something. It may lessen the mortification to know that it was a *sancudos* or a *culex pipiens* that had out-manœuvred you, your punkah, and your curtains of net, and not an ordinary vulgar "mosquito," but it would not lessen the irritation. The thing we call a mosquito would bite as hard by any other name, and with regard to their horrid persons enough is known already. It is sufficient that they look gaunt and empty before sitting down on you, and that after dinner they look quite the reverse,—fat, fozy, and plethoric. Physically, they seem to be at least of two kinds, the one drab-coloured and the other speckled, each as bad as the other, but much worse. Morally, their divisions are legion, and a musically inclined pachyderm might reasonably expect to find the full octave among them. Even the unmusical can detect individuals by their tone. There is the speckled baritone brute that rushes at you from the other end of the garden, and with three trumpet notes proceeds to drill a hole into you, and usually gets killed for his clumsiness; for he settles on you with a confiding flop that would do credit to an able-bodied fly. But he is far preferable to the miscreant that skulks and dances behind your head for half an hour, leaving you to suspect that it has settled on your ear only by the sudden cessation of its exasperating sing-song in a minor key. Some are too ravenous even to roar at you before beginning dinner, and blind with their horrid lust for food, pitch down on the first corner of you or your clothes that they come to, without a thought of grace. But they are less hateful than the dawdling dilettanti, which hover undecidedly about your ears or the nape of your neck, whining an obligato recitative in C sharp; or the others that trifle in a falsetto with your ankles. Straightforward honest wickedness is at all times better than underhanded villainy. Therefore, of the two mosquitoes that come with the fixed purpose of eating you, that is the lesser criminal which begins first. He is more pardonable than the procrastinating villain, who, however long his grace before meat may be, and however indifferent and careless his demeanour, will, you know, ultimately attain his end and satisfy his hunger out of sight—and probably out of reach. There is no sinner so bad as a tedious one, and the worst part of a mosquito bite is the lively apprehension of it. Some one has said that it is while he is waiting for Calcraft to let him drop that society is revenged on the murderer, and this is true. The fly does not object to being eaten by the spider; he expected that. But what he hates is being wrapped up in web, like a parcel, beforehand.

By analogy I conclude that the mosquito which comes to bite you, and bites you without more ado, is not so execrable as the other which comes to bite you and keeps you waiting while it sings its catechism.

Part IV.

UNDER THE TREES.

UNDER THE TAMARIND.
UNDER THE MANGO.
UNDER THE PEEPUL.
UNDER THE BAMBOOS.
UNDER THE BANYAN.

UNDER THE TAMARIND

OT all the pines of Pan, the bleak-grown pines wind-haunted, nor Athene's olives,

> "The holy bloom whose hoar leaf
> High in the shrine of Pandrosus
> Hath honour of us all"

in the city of the Violet Crown: nor the eternal holly of old Saturn, the broad-shaded oaks of Zeus, nor the laurels of the

> "God of the golden bow
> And of the golden lyre,
> God of the golden hair
> And of the golden fire;

nor yet the myrtles of Her whom the ancients worshipped in gardens, citron groves her shrines and passing sweet her altars of

> "Pansies and violets and asphodel
> And hyacinths; earth's freshest and greenest lap;"

no, nor any other tree that has claimed the admiration

of men, from the maples of the West to the cedars of the East, may vie for "the chiefdom of green groves" with the Tamarind.

Under the tamarind then, the goodly tree that hangs over the bank where the shrunken river, "pale with the sere leaves shaken upon her from her own trees," goes querulous over the upstart rocks which in the days of her rain-weather plenty were smothered deep under her flood. But now that she has fallen upon narrow days, each pebble thrusts up its head to fret the languid stream. Perched among them the marbled kingfisher contemplates at his full-stomached leisure the intervals of water in which the bewildered fishlets circle an unwonted course, wondering where may be the opening into that spacious river that used to run down to the sea. Hard by, his legs showing a cubit above the weeds in the shallows, the pied crane "arbiter of the terraqueous swamp" goes daintily, while the efts *ranæque palustres* lurking close, mark the thin shadows that in the setting sun straddle across the stream.

Down into the west the red-horsed chariot of Agni has carried the Fire-god—all vain his pursuit of the disdainful Night. And already the amber clouds that had rolled up, ethereal dust, from under his hurrying wheels are paling into grey before the mocking moon. The night wind is already up, fluttering the dry siris-pods, showering down the sissoo's little leaves, and setting all the tamarind tips gossiping in whispers. And away down the reach of the river a mist is gathering—which the river, and which the mist? Ay, which the solid earth, and which the running river? How easy to fancy shrouded in that mist some river thing—shrouded as was Satan when he floated over the walls of Paradise, a vague mist, to tempt our parents. No Parthenope or graceful Sabrina who

> " Oft at eve
> Visits the herds along the twilight meadows,
> Healing all urchin blasts and ill-luck signs
> That the shrewd meddling elf delights to make : "

nor other gentle Nereid, Arthur's sister with her hands pearl-filled for luckless fishers or silver-slippered Thetis with her home in the Sea and her heart on the Earth—but some fateful river thing, death-bearing, sickness its melancholy gift. How easily can it, all unsuspected, rise from the river's ooze, and concealed by its own miasma drapery, pass over to the shore, creep up the dal-covered slope, and gathering its mist-skirts closer together, fill the hamlet yonder with its penetrating presence, pausing at each open door to distribute its gifts of fever and palsied death. How aptly have men spoken of "the mist of the Past!" Look back now into the distance, where, be sure, are growing just such trees as we ourselves are standing under, are living just such things as we. Here and there a Homer-tree or Troy-rock looms out through or above the vapour, but where are the nations of smaller things that so lately made all that space populous? Nearer to us the outlines are not blurred yet, and across the bend of the stream the moonlight with its gracious alchemy has thrown a sparkling strip of shimmering gold for the elves who wish to cross the river and has turned to silver all the bubbles that break upon the stones. And then in the moth-time the bats come down from the fissured rocks, chittering as they go, to skim the pools, and the night heron, surely the ghostliest of fowls, sends his cry along the sedges in reply—oh! gruesome antiphony—to the horned owl's ululation. Scrambling about in the peepul-tree beyond, the flying fox, that "thing of dark imaginings," scatters the clustered berries, or with unseemly squeakings foregathers for clumsy scuffle with his kind. I doubt if their lives were on edition properly revised.

High over head glitters Orion, armed as when he vexed the Red Sea coast to overthrow "Busiris and his Memphian chivalry," his dagger unsheathed and the diamonds of his belt complete. Along the horizon the spangled Hydra waves his sinuous length. Sirius calls across the void to his brother star, and Berenice has shaken out all her golden tresses. In high galaxy all the stars are ranged—Perseus of the doughty sword, and near him, the sundered chains still pendant from her wrists, Andromeda scarce snatched from death; with his lion's fell about him great Hercules and, paw uplift, the mighty Bear. His wings a-glitter, Pegasus circles his brilliant course, the Eagle its broad-feathered pinions stretched before it, hardly gaining on his flight, and the Swan, star-crowned, left far behind.

How fast asleep that palm is!—leaning over as if with nodding head. So softly has the light stolen in between the stems that not a frond has waked, and on the ground the shadows of its great spiked leaves lie as clean cut as the still leaves themselves. The bair-tree close by droops its fruited branches to the ground and, enmeshed with tangling gourds, holds in its pavilion a family of drowsy birds. A night-mare—the vision of a dream weasel climbing stealthily up the easy tree—awakes a sleeper, but moving uneasily he feels on either side his feathered companion in the close-packed row, and settles again to his sleep, and a chirp of satisfaction goes down the roosting line. "All's well!" But hush! From out the dark dal crop has stealthily leapt a wolf, and standing stone-still on the mud wall, now shows against the moon-track on the water like a figure cast in bronze. Hush! the wolf, so the peasant legends say, strikes dumb those on whom in moonlight it turns its face, and "wolf madness" supervenes. So let it look across the river. But why should that stealthy white-toothed brute have been sacred to Mars? Swift only to pursue; cowardly before an enemy; bold only as a dexterous thief is bold; lurking by day in ditches where it maddens to hear pass bleating by the flocks it dare not attack, but forward under cover of night to fill the deserted highway with its complaining voice. What has this brute to do with the chivalrous God of War? Where is it now? The mere rustle of a foolish flying-fox in the peepul-tree startled it, and like a shadow the grim beast of prey has slipt back into the covert of the dal. And the suddenness of its going makes the night seem more blank than ever.

Look overhead at the sky. Clouds are driving along it, and the moon, now in eclipse, now shining full, passes alternate from a prison to a throne. Now gulfed in a dark spasm, now queening it in rounded splendour. And none to triumph with her but you and me, the flying foxes, the Endymion-bartavelle, and the owls. Athene Brahma!—what a name for a chuckling owlet! for the bird that one has spoken of as "very ridiculous and imitative, which while it dances, wagging its head from side to side, the fowlers snare," and which in Milton's sonnet is lumped with "cuckoos, asses, apes, and dogs" as conspirators in "barbarous noise." Hear what Aristotle has to say of it: "The crow and the owl are enemies, for at mid-day the crow taking advantage of the dim sight of the owl, secretly seizes its eggs and devours them, and the owl eats those of the crow during the night, and one of them is master by day, the other by night. The owl and the orchilus are also enemies, for the latter eats the eggs of the owl. During the day other birds fly round the owl which is called 'astonishing it,' and as they fly round it pluck off its feathers." This of Athene Brahma! "And the owl," they say, "was a baker's daughter." All night long she sate up to get ready the little loaves that on their way to their toil the workmen would call in for at daybreak, and only fresh from the oven would they have them. And so, when all the world else had just risen from bed to begin the day, the baker's daughter was blinking with sleep. But though owl-like, why was she actually turned into an owl? Have you heard the legend?

It was in the days when Pan was king of all the country side, that Hermes, bound on private business to Poros by the blue Ægean, was pacing wearily along the stony road. The cicalas shrilled to him from the dusty arbutus bushes and Helios, curious of his object, stared after him with all his might, and Hermes was very hot. His caduceus cunningly wisped with oaten straw seemed but a common staff. Under clumsy sandals his dipterous heels went unsuspected, and tucked up beneath his broad-brimmed hat the golden locks—Maia's pride—lay snug. He seemed but a bucolic agriote, a comely lad enough, going up, it might be, to give account to his master of the farm upon the Didymian hill. At a turn of the road he came upon a baker's stall, and dozing under the awning sate, blinking at the sunlight, the baker's daughter, a round faced, mealy wench. And right tempting to the thirsty god looked the cool grape clusters and the Persic peaches in their amber syrup. But he had no money. So trusting to his comely face to get him a bunch of grapes, he stopped before the stall. The round-faced one only blinked. "I am very hot," said he, and "Ugh!" replied the drowsy wench, "And very thirsty," and "Ugh!" said she. "Will you give me a bunch of grapes?" smiled he, but "Ugh! ugh!" was all she gave. At which the handsome god lost temper (tantæne!) and moved away, but hearing a sleepy chuckle behind him, turned his head in hope. But "Ugh!" said she. "Ugh! ugh!" retorted he, "ay, Ugh! ugh! for aye, and proper language enough for you. You do not like the sun? So be it." But "Ugh!" again said she. Then Hermes went on to Poros, hotter than ever, cursing the sun that shone, the cicalas that shrilled, and the lizards that basked on the stones; but in the cool evening, with Hesperus overhead, he passed again the corner where stood the baker's stall. And on the awning-pole there sate a round-faced, blinking bird. "Ugh," cried the god to the owl; and "Ugh! ugh!" replied the baker's daughter.

I'll be bound you never heard that legend before.

UNDER THE MANGO.

IT was just here in the dark shade of the mango that they laid the body down—the strong dead hands full of water-weeds, the fair hair still tangled with the river growth. The old tree throws a grave shade, you see. Its deep canopy is solemn enough for even the august presence of death.

It is an idle story, perhaps, but even though you may not have any superstitious belief in coincidences, it may interest you the while we loiter here under the sombre tree.

A. and two friends were building for themselves a shooting bungalow on the bank of the river K. at N. ; but one day—the house was then some six feet above the foundations—when they had ridden over from their tents to see how the work got on, they found an old man, a Mahomedan, sitting by a bone heap, and filling the air with his lamentations. On asking the cause of his grief, the old man said that the spot on which the house was being built, was the burial-ground of his family, and insisted on the house being pulled down, and all the bones that had been turned up replaced. This, as the man admitted he had no claim to the land, they refused to do, and so at last he went away, but complaining still. To celebrate the completion of their "shooting-box," A. and his friends asked a party over from cantonments, and all went merrily. After dinner they adjourned to the verandah to smoke. It was an exquisite night. The hot weather was coming on, true enough, but there was a pleasant breeze from across the river fluttering the stiff mango leaves into whispers, and in the still air could be heard from the jungle beyond the river the hoot of the distant owl, or from the scattered *khets*, the bark of the prowling fox. The sky above was thick with stars, and the clear moonlight gave that white frosty look to everything that so often mocks us in the hot weather.

Lazily stretched on their bedding, the smokers were drowsily talking over to-morrow's plans, when suddenly—so suddenly that he seemed to some of them to have risen from the ground—there appeared before them a white-clothed figure. The head was uncovered and closely shaven, but the white beard told his age, and brought back to mind the old man they had found by the bones. In one hand he held a skull. And for some moments there was silence, the white figure standing motionless in the clear moonlight with both arms stretched out before him, and in one hand the skull. And then all suddenly, as when a sluice-gate yielding lets the water through with a rush, the old man burst out, " On the skulls of my fathers I curse you, you three who have built this house upon their graves. And with my tongue all the dead whom you have outraged curse you. Before the fruit is again on the mango-tree you shall die, you three who built this house. Your deaths shall be sudden, and your graves in this country. As for this house, it shall not outlive you. *Accursed!*" With the last word he flung the skull from him, and turning round walked up to the very edge of the river bank. And whether the bank gave way under him or he flung himself over it, was hard to say. Nor in the noise of the swirl of the water as it swept round the bluff did they hear any splash of his fall. But he was gone none the less. The body did not run the gauntlet of the crocodiles: at any rate it was never found, and the police could give no clue as to who the man was.

"And the coincidences? when did *they* begin?"

"They began at once. All three died within the year, and the house was washed clean away. A. was the last." He was a strong man and a capital swimmer, and the distance was nothing. But he never reached the shore. Cramp must have seized him, for on a sudden he went under without a cry. The body was intercepted down at the ford yonder, and the body, till we arrived, was laid here under this tree. You do not believe in coincidences? Perhaps not, but the story is true.

Not that the mango is altogether a tree of sad memories. It has joyous traditions and as honourable as most. Indeed, few vegetables can claim such honours as the mango—except perhaps those botanical impostors, "the amaranth, the asphodel and moly." Many no doubt have just cause for pride. The oak, with its thousand memories of Druid and Dryad, of Epirote priestess and green-kirtled outlaw, of Cavalier-king and Hebrew Prince; "that same tree, in which Demophoön, By his disloyalty lamented sore, Eternal hurt left unto many one,"—the tree of "the Mighty Seaman," and of happy Pan "oak haunting." The plane-trees of Hippocrates, and the sycamores (friend of little men) of the Academe of the broad-shouldered philosopher. The mulberries stirred by God's own hand to be ominous of coming victory, honoured even now at Stratford with wreath, and dance, and song, and still held holy in Athens. The palm-trees of the trumpet-shaken city, or that one beneath which the wife of Lapidoth gave law to the tribes of Palestine, and which afterwards became the solitary emblem of Judæa captive. The shittim, the cedar, and the box; "the sweet cypresse, signe of deadly bale;" the laurel, pine, olive, and myrtle—all the groves of the bright gods of Greece; Hiawatha's birch, that painful tree; the hawthorn of the Saint; the tree that bears the nest of "that self-begotten bird, in the Arabian woods embost;" the kalki, "watcher and guard of the graves of the dead;" the asoca, that blossoms when touched by a woman's foot; the sad Cassia of Freemasonry; the Upas; the tree which the grape-vine loves; "the black holme;" the yew, heroic on many a splendid field; the fig-tree, which the Athenians revered and all fateful for doomed Messene; the great lindens of the Hyperborean garden, where, beyond the cold touch of the North, the poet sate to sing, what time the fight raged fiercely, that filled Etzel's halls with slaughter; the elm, of all trees sad, the aspen of all woods holy; the fir-tree, which the stork consecrates; and "the rougher-rinded pine, The great Argoan ship's great ornament;" the conscious hazel, leaping in the wizard's hand; "and eke those trees in whose transformed hew, The Sunne's sad daughters wayld the rash decay Of Phaëton;" the elder, whose brittle bough betrayed the betrayer of our Lord; the juniper, wholesome only to the wearied Tishbite, fatal to all else; the pomegranate, that shaded Saul's eventful sleeping; the vengeful ash, hoary in traditions; the sâl, beneath which Buddha passed into Nirvana. Think of these and many others, all the trees of story—from the lowly willows of the brook, drooping still with the heavy memories of Jewish harps, to that awful vegetable, "Eden's dread probationary tree," "the tree of prohibition, root of all our woe"—and with any one of them the mango holds its own. While as yet in Europe the brute was lord of the man, Asia taught in her schools an old mythology with legends of feast, and bird, and tree, and among them all the mango had honour. It was "the tree" of one of the Seven Continents; and in Swarga, the Paradise of Indra, the mango bloomed as one of the sacred five. Surely honour enough! Nor the cedars of Lebanon nor the oaks of Dodona can claim more. And in happy memories the mango is as rich as the roses of Horace or Hafez, or the myrtles of the Paphian. Have you never read "The Song of the Koel?"[1] It begins:—

> "O youths and maidens, rise and sing!
> The koel is come who leads the spring:
> The buds that were sleeping his voice have heard,
> And the tale is borne on by each nesting bird.
>
> The trees of the forest have all been told,
> They have donn'd their mantles of scarlet and gold,
> To welcome him back they are bravely dress'd,
> But he loves the blossoming mango best.
>
> The koel is come, glad news to bring!
> On the blossoming mango he rests his wing.
> Though its hues may be dull, it is sweet, oh sweet;
> And its shade and its fruit the wanderer greet."

And then goes on to tell how Kama, the Cupid of India, "the bodiless god who reigns above," distressed for the sons of men that they were so sorely vexed by Taraka the demon, offered his aid to work out the oracle's decree, that help should come from sonless Shiva's son. But on Himavan's side, Shiva the recluse, loveless and unlovely, lay among the ashes.

> "He moved not, nor spoke, save in telling his beads
> On the rosary strung of the jungle seeds,"

---

[1] *Indian Ballads*, W. Waterfield, C.S., 1868.

and against him in vain young Kama was emptying his quiver of its arrows blossom-barbed, for the awful god was proof against shafts that suffice to consume the hearts of mortals. But the love-god only laughed as he took from his side the last, the mango-headed arrow, and

> "Oh! sharp is the arrowy blossom's smart,
> For the mango flower ne'er miss d the heart;
> And the work of the gods is fairly done,
> And help shall arise out of Shiva's son."

Ay, under the mangos! All day long to sit and watch the ripening fruit, to wage a perpetual war with little beasts and little birds, every squirrel a throe, and each finch a spasm. Wearied with doing nothing, thinking nothing, desperate of sleep, starting up to shout at every parrot that shows a disposition to wheel round the tree, to have to make a frantic demonstration in the direction of every squirrel. The day is haunted by suspicions of tree-cats among the fruit, and with the stars there rise nightmares of persistent flying-foxes. Life has many dreary phases, but surely none more drab than this, to gutter old age away sitting on a charpoy from early dawn—

> "The morning cool when from ready pool
> Up springs the whistling crane"

—until

> "Plaintive through the twilight air
> Is heard the curlew's cry;"

to watch another's fruit a-ripening, to see the sun rise

and no day's doings to set about, merely to turn on the charpoy and shout up vaguely into the tree overhead, to wait through the lagging hours—nothing to do but to shout again at a venture now and then, to see the moon rise without the bartavelle's satisfaction of eating the moon-beams, to wake all the night through, with all the patience but none of the sweet solace of the Brahmini duck. Surely, nothing can be more dreary than this, the lot of the watcher beneath the mangos. All day long, there pass along the high road friends with friends, but to the old woman under the tree the hot wind carries only the dust that their feet stir up. The parrots fly up and away again by their households and parishes, and every squirrel has its mate close by. And all night long, the owlets chuckle together among themselves, and are merry, the dissipated koel needs no more company than the wife he screams to, and the jackals are a-mirth together. But for the beldame under the tree, her one meal eaten, what diversion is there? Three trees off is another cripple on another charpoy, and midway between the two a pariah dog sits scratching itself all day long. And all night it yap-yaps, but why, to save its life it could not tell you, at another pariah dog that, in the extreme distance, goes on yap-yaping too, each hoping, perhaps, to have the last word. Every dog, they say, has his day. If so, this dog can hardly have had his yet. Perhaps he will have it next week. Perhaps he has had it already,—so long go that he has forgotten all about it, and believes that he was always the dingy, dusty thing he is. Littered in a box he thought at first that the world was square, and lined with grass, but falling out one day he found himself in error, and in a larger world, four walled still, but lined smooth with mud, and in one corner he found a bundle of faggots, in another a spinning-wheel, in a third some brazen utensils somewhat savoury smelling to his puppy notions, and in the fourth, a confusion of rags with ten toes. He counted them each one sticking out at one end, and a fuzzy head sticking out at the other, and it all smelt much the same. Inspirited by this adventurous exploration, he tried an unwieldly gambol, but his legs, unsteady beneath him, betrayed him into a lurch against the wall, and lo! it gave with his weight, and head over heels the puppy rolled out through the mat-door and down three steps into the open air. And there a dog bit him.

> "So rounds he to a separate mind
> From whence clear memory may begin,
> As through the frame that binds him in
> His isolation grows defined."

But though experience fast enriched him in worldly wisdom, he has never forgotten the hands that picked him up from where he lay that day, a dusty, weak-legged, bitten puppy, at the bottom of the steps—and so, wherever the old hands go, the dog goes too. To-day he is with her as she watches beneath the mangos. And while she shouts he scratches.

UNDER THE PEEPUL.

UNDER the peepul by the ruined well. The peepul is sacred among the natives, and yet they call it "the treacherous friend." And well they may. Planted at first partly to propitiate some hamlet deity, partly for the sake of the shelter it would give to the drawers of water, the peepul for some years repaid the villagers with grateful shade. But at last it grew old and strong, and, conscious that its sturdy roots had struck deep into the earth, basely turned upon the sons of those who had set it there, and driving its gnarled feet against the feeble masonry of the well, thrust it from its place. And one morning, coming to the well with their poised pyramids of pots, the women found the rope all too short to reach the water. The peepul, far down below the water-level, had breached the well, and the water as it rose drained off to either side, while through the opening—traitor's work—the soil silted in. And so, after long consultations, the well was abandoned.

"He doth cast abroad the fitches and scatter the cummin-seed and cast in the principal wheat, and the appointed barley and the rye, in their places." So runs the quaint English of our Bible. Then, no doubt, the hand that broadcast sows the fitches also grafted this strange growth of vegetables in the well? What a world it is, this well! Close to the brink, where a stone has been displaced by the peepul's roots, a troglodyte lizard, "the foe of spiders," as Aristotle calls it, has made its home—the tail that protrudes has a possessive complexion about it that speaks the householder with vested interests. Much lower down is another hole, and in it nests the blue pigeon. To one side, close by the tuft of maiden's hair fern, you may mark a wasp's papery nest; and in the mud, fathoms down, is a monastery of frogs. And how did they get there? To say that they were born there, only throws the problem a generation back, and to suppose that they went there of their free agency is to think frogs fools. I never had it explained to me as I could wish, the why and the wherefore of these ascetic frogs. In the tank yonder, bristling with *singharas*, I can imagine frog-life enjoyable enough, for, after all, paddy-birds are fallible; but down at the bottom of a well, even with Truth for a companion, life would, I think, soon stale. But they are well out of the way, these " tuneful natives of the reedy lake."

In Cyrene once, as in Abdera, there were no frogs; but, as erst to plague-vexed Egypt, "the croaking nuisance" was sent, they say, in punishment. Nor is it wonderful that to explain the presence within their borders of the hateful batrachian, nations should thus have gone out of their way to imagine the spite of a vengeful god. And when frogs jump, or fall, or are dropped down empty wells, men are justified in glee. None the less, such life must be most monotonous and very undesirable.

So certainly thinks that sparrow, vagabond among birds.

> " Under the changeful sky,
> Who so free in the land,
> Who so contented as I.
> Cheerful I hop, by wayward fancy led,
> Trusting in God, who the sparrows still hath fed."

And what may that individual sparrow be doing here so far from the dwellings of man? But what might they have been doing in Tobit's wall, or what business have they in half their haunts—these contemners of the God of Boundaries, impartial Terminus. I have never spoken well of the sparrow, " the meanest of the feathered race;" and might quote from what I have written elsewhere, much to his discredit. But my phials of wrath are as deep as any of the Apocalypse, and I willingly believe, with Sir Thomas Browne, that this assertive bird, " stiff in opinion, always in the wrong," has only arrived at the dignity of being concerned in the leper-cleansing ceremonial of Mosaic law by some accident of translation. On its merits, the sparrow stands formally damned. And adventitious claims to favour it has none. Some birds have at stated periods of the year a keen intelligence and "sharp apprehension" of poverty, and we do not resent their overtures, as with the English robin,—

> " Who never can seem to intrude,
> Though in all places equally free."

But the sparrow is always too well fed to make his familiarities tolerable. From his persistence, however, has arisen on our side a sulky acquiescence in his impudence, and from this he argues his own importance, that he is always welcome, and, indeed, inseparable from the world's welfare. As if the cobwebs on it helped to support the roof!

The mynas have a nest in the peepul, and it belongs to all the parish. It is as much common property as our church steeple. And surely nothing could be less private than that. The lugger falcon has its nest between the pilasters that hold up the clock, while in the corresponding slit a blue jay is rearing its gape-mouthed brood; on the top, a kite is always on the watch, and in the niche below an owl dozes away its days. And yet there is always plenty of room on our steeple for crows, green parrots, and sparrows. So with the myna's nest in the peepul. All day long, and every day, the mynas go flying about with straws a yard long trailing from their beaks, and they talk to each other in a sanguine way as they tuck the ends into the heap of rubbish they are collecting in the fork of the tree, and which they call their nest. Sometimes one of them sits at home on guard while the other goes foraging; but oftener both are away together, busy in some knuckle end of a garden, tugging straws and strings out of a dust-heap. Meanwhile, three crows are criticizing the tag-rag nest, and turning it up with their beaks, for they are possessed with the idea that the mynas only affect nidification as a pretext for concealing a treasure of bones. And they have some grounds for their suspicions, for once it happened that one of the mynas, in its zeal to add to the nest-heap, contributed the dried foot of a fowl, and the crow that discovered the cache was chased about the garden till sun-down by all his tribe. The foot dropped ultimately into a water-butt, and for the rest of the evening all the crows sate bickering round the edge. The myna's nesting, moreover, saves the uxorious sparrow much toil, for the harder the mynas work the larger grows the sparrow's frowsy nursery. The shikra hawk, too, looks in upon the mynas as he passes of a morning, to see if there are any young ones fit to be eaten yet; and when no one else is occupying it, the squirrel lounges on the platform, to exchange frivolous gossip with a comrade on the fallen pillar of the well.

See—the lizard has come up to bask in the sun. Some of my acquaintances affect to like lizards, and when they are busy with white ants the small saurian certainly has some claim upon our respect. But there is too much affectation about the lizard to make him altogether admirable. In the first place, his laborious assumption of a thoughtful demeanour. Pretending to be abstracted in deepest cogitation, he will remain motionless on your wall by the hour together, and I deny, with Christopher North, that any man has a right " to leave his carcase in a room without a mind to belong to it." To be absent-minded, is popularly held to be an amiable weakness, whereas it should be condemned, for when it is natural it is in the great majority of cases only the expression of a general tendency to wool-gather, and when it is assumed, it is an impertinence. For assumed it certainly is at times, just as a melancholy demeanour is cultivated, that the world may mistake Jacques for a poet. Again, the lizard moves with a slow and well-considered step, to have it understood that he is no fool, but, as Bacon says, we should not argue a man wise because he goes cautiously; it is when men are in the dark that they walk most delicately. Yet the lizard was worshipped in Egypt —but then the merry Egyptians worshipped paddy-birds and beetles and onions. More wonderful is it that the lizard should have found a place among the constellations. But perhaps Lacerta was of some uncommon kind, some iguana of the Brazils, or saurian of that lizard's paradise, Arabia the Stony, or, even perhaps, one of the inform amphibians that trailed along the prediluvian slime. Anyhow, the lizard on the well there had better go back to his hole, for here come the monkeys from the village grain-shop, "apes with foreheads villainous low," who will eat him if they catch him. They come here every afternoon for a gossip, and as evening closes in they creep up one by one to their roost on the smooth, level boughs of the peepul.

Few animals have fallen in with so much ill-treatment at the hands of men of science as the monkey. But the reason is not far to seek. The savant resents the resemblance of the Simian to himself. So he carefully collects all the facts within reach that bear hardly on the monkey.

> "Their own defects invisible to them,
> Seen in another, they at once condemn;
> And, though self-idolized in every case,
> Hate their own likeness in a brother's face."

He therefore sets the monkey forward as the most abandoned of God's creatures, punishing his innocent likeness to himself by spitefully slurring over his good points. The jackal is detestable altogether, but what naturalist omits to say in his defence that he is "most useful"? We in India credit him with only a very moderate degree of utility, for we know that the kites and vultures would do his work for him with pleasure at any time and with less noise. Again, the cock-roach who pretends to eat bugs, but prefers boots, the savant has for him a good word always. But then neither the jackal nor the cock-roach presume to resemble the writer. The monkey does. So to punish his presumption he is written down treacherous, mischievous, and dirty. For pure shame they allow him the virtues of affection for offspring and sagacity in self-preservation, universal in Nature,—the ostrich only excepted :—

> "Silliest of the feather'd kind,
> And form'd of God without a parent's mind."

His very agility is made light of by Buffon, and so bitter are they against him, that if they could they would, I believe, deny that his tail is ever prehensile. This meanness is not commendable. The monkey, let them write what they may, had no finger in his own construction. The great Editor sent him no proofs of himself to revise. He was not asked for an opinion, but came into his present state anthropomorphoid nilly willy, and if the truth were known, rather nilly than willy I fancy. For I cannot believe that the monkey is proud of his resemblance to us. If he is, his head is easily turned. The monkey, I take it, is ashamed of his postulatory resemblance to man. While you watch him, intense dejection is his chief characteristic. He is sad-faced and contemplative. He begins vacantly to scratch the earth. After a while, he affects an interest in a very reasonable manner, as if looking for something beneath the surface; and you say, "How like a human being!" The monkey suddenly stops scratching, and turning his back upon the spot which so recently seemed to interest him, gazes into space; and you laugh and say, "How like a monkey!" So perhaps, after all, the distance between you and him is not so very great, and some of his sins may be found to be your sins also. At any rate he is as sensible as that half-witted son of his whom your bearer has juggled into your domestic staff as his "help." "An idiot" is he? I make no doubt of it he is, but there is no need to jeer at him for that.

Misfortune is not always the echo of iniquity, nor the very shadow of sin. Perhaps if he had learned less or loved less, he might have been sane now, or perhaps he was in the flood-tide of success with a strong brain carving out his way to fame "when mortality pulled him by the ear." His body is now a habitation tenantless, an Athens with its Acropolis full of owls, Palmyra a wilderness of raving jackals. No, do not jeer at him, one of "God's children," as the poor call the mad. Are you sure your own horoscope is not in Saturn, the Lord of Melancholy? And have you counted the convolutions of your own cerebullum, to feel so confident that you yourself are in no need of the white-flowered herb of Anticyra? After all he is not more ugly than Socrates, nor so wicked as you or I.

UNDER THE BAMBOOS.

HE is an old man who can say, "I have seen the bamboo flower twice," for the bamboo flowers but once in thirty years, and when it has flowered, it dies. The swan sings but once "the sad dirge of its certain ending," and dies.

"The whale, too, (remarkable coincidence!) only yields its blubber once—and when it does, it dies."

"Yes, W., you are right. And like the whale, the bamboo compensates for the singularity of its autumn by the profligate profusion of its one harvest, and to the banquet, as to some *Volksfest* in a year of Jubilee, flock the nations of living things." At Behemoth's obsequies the air is clamorous with ravenous fowl "the sea-mew's clang," and petrels, the scavengers of the wave, "plaining discrepant between sea and sky." And all round the bulky death gleam sharks, vulture-minded, their white bellies gleaming through the oil-stained water as they turn beneath the floating offal, and, shoaling round, the finny things of the deep sea hold a universal picnic. And so with the bamboo, for when the great grass is seeding, dying, the beasts tell it to the birds, and from the birds the insects hear it. From his hill-coverts paces down the stately sambhur, and the jungle undergrowth sends forth the silent deer. Out from his lair among the rocks the wild boar leads his bristly household, and up the ravine sides with rustling quills climbs the careful porcupine. Plunging with commotion of leaves from tree to tree the monkeys come along in their tribes and families. The wary nilghai is tempted to the feast. In squadrons the rats troop in, long-tailed and short—an exodus of rodents, such as the astonished traveller sometimes meets in Western Savannahs and Central Asian Steppes. By their battalions the field-ravaging mice—a mouse-invasion such as entrapped that hapless bishop by the Rhine. From tree and bush and brake, the birds flock noisily together to this great carnival of Pan, not—

> "As when the total kind
> Of birds, in orderly array on wing
> Came summon'd over Eden to receive
> Their names of Adam;"

but in all the unscientific confusion of the fifth day, when at the word the "tepid caves and fens and shores" gave forth their miscellaneous broods, a mob of chattering, twittering things, a very wilderness of feathers.

Under the bamboos is now scattered a complete Order,

all the families of the grain-eating birds. Jungle fowl, spurred and quarrelsome,—

> " And that other whose gay train
> Adorns him, colour'd with the florid hues
> Of rainbows and starry eyes,' "

that " sumptuous Pharisee," the " self-applauding peacock," who

> " Treads as if, some solemn music near,
> His measured step were govern'd by his ear,
> And seems to say ' Ye meaner fowl, give place ! '
> I am all splendour, dignity, and grace."

Partridges and quails in number, as if the Hebrews were again on their travels: sleek doves whose plumage as they move glints a dozen colours, and finches—all the twittering crew. Such a gathering that the owl wakes up to listen ! And all the aviary is at food together. Each beak that opens to take in a seed lets fall a sound. And still the grain keeps showering down, for every bird that perches on or flies off the bamboo's drooping stems, scatters a rain of seed upon the feeding crowd below. The timid doves rise startled at every shower, and at the first sound of their clapping pinions, the whole gathering with a multitudinous flurry of wings rise all together, baring the seed-strewn ground. Once round the clump they wheel, and then hungrily re-settle with nervous chattering to the feast. And so the whole day through—a Babel of feathered things, now jostling on the ground, and again in sudden panic darkening the air. Nor is man backward to claim his share of the bamboo's bounty. From the hamlets round, like ant-files, the people all day long thread their way through crop and scrub, each child at one journey storing as much as its father might win from the stubborn glebe in twelve hours' toil. And yet there is enough and to spare for "the parsimonious emmet." Its grass-bare tracks already radiate from the bamboo clump to every point of the jungle round, and for weeks to come the long, black lines of diligent insects will stretch from barn to field.

Surely the bamboo's carnival—

> Beneath the open sky she spreads the feast
> 'Tis free to all—

free as the landscape—may rank with all the chiefest of the wonders of Nature—the multitudinous nesting of sea-birds, the flowering of the Talipot palm, the animal marvels of the primeval forests of the Amazons, the butterfly migrations that have amazed travellers from all time, the Northern Lights, the coral islands of the Southern seas,—or any other of the *chefs-d'œuvre* of Nature, those miracles of the created world that cripple language and defy the pen. But we have seen as yet only the opening of the Carnival. The close is very different. The Shadows of Death are falling on the riotous crew.

Far and near the Raptores have marked the hurrying flights of the grain-eating fowl, and whither tending, and now "like Ate hot from hell" the birds of prey sweep up the sky to the scene of the thoughtless revel. Beneath the bamboos they surprise the gluttonous crew. First, the daring shikra, with arrowy flight upon a quail cluster bent, scatters for a minute the feeding family; but while beneath the babool close by he sits to tear his prey, the rest return to the feast, heedless of repeated losses. The fine-winged peregrines glide, swift as Ariels, from the neighbouring thicket and, hardly checking their flight as they pick up a bird, slip without flap of wings through the bamboo clump and at each ghost-shadow flitting over them, the partridges cluck uneasily, but, though there is one of them the less, the rest feed on. Anon the shahin, "the Royal Falcon" of the East, disdaining concealment in its approach, pierces the air before it with a cry, a very dagger-stroke of sound, and hurtling through the rustling brake, bursts in like a shell upon the heedless throng. The whole revel startled, is on the wing at once, and through and through the wheeling flights, like arrows among a running foe, dart the keen-winged hawks, and when the revellers are at their tables again, the air is flecked with feathers that float down, mementos disregarded, upon the chattering feast. Here the bold laggar wheels to choose, and then, stooping, drops like a falling meteor upon the quarry, and, burdened, wings a heavy flight along the ground. The merlin, sworn foe of jays, shrills angrily from the covert of the dak, where he crouches to tear a dove, as the goshawk, spoil-laden too, wavers in the air above it half minded to alight. Fluttering the finches, the sparrow-hawks skim in and out, and the red-legged falcons, the swallow hunters, desolate many a sylvan choir. Nor are these all, for "in the emptier waste resembing air, weighs his spread wings" the Olympian eagle, waiting till some youngling shall tempt the open ground to shoot, swift as Krishna's quoit, to earth. And see here, a desolation round it, the glutton buzzard feasting where it struck its prey, too ravenous to heed the stealthy harrier, the cat among birds, that, silent as a thought, has passed in a flash of feathers between it and the brake. And sulking on the mohwa-tree, the vultures—"Pharoah's chickens!" —wait for the carnival to end, that they may clean the board. But they will wait in vain. Till sundown the mad debauch goes on, and then with noiseless flight the downy owls, awaking to perception of the scene that all day long has puzzled their blinking wits, float through the shade and many a rat and mouse will go *apud inferos*, and many a pellet of fur will strew the ground to-morrow. And last, through the gloaming, paces forth on velvet paw the lord of the jungle, and then woe to the feeding deer!

And so, the death of things the oil that works her wheels, Nature proceeds. The fleshless laughter of the grave supervenes on the merriment of the living, and from out blue skies breaks the flame that scorches and scathes and kills. A terrible idyll enough, though the actors are but birds and beasts! One day, happy thankful creatures jostling at a feast bounteously spread, as in Eden, for all that chose to come, and the next, as again in Eden, let loose upon them all the butchers of the skies and jungles. Historical analogies suggest themselves readily, but the final scene first perhaps recalls (to compare a small thing with a great) that most appalling chapter in the history of any people, the carnage by the Tengis Lake as told by De Quincey's terrible pen in his "Revolt of the Tartars."

Ay, each has to dodge Death for himself. Do you hear me, you hoopoe there, so busy with that reluctant worm? The world is not so over-ready to help you if you do not help yourself. The tethered kid would run some risk of being forgotten and left in the orchard all night if it abandoned itself to mute despair. But its importunate bleating calls help to it at last, and from within the safe enclosure of the house it hears securely the hungry chorus of the jackal pack as they sweep by under the guavas. What insect among yon myriads will help this ant, trying to drag over a root the half of a wasp it has found? It has wandered far from its kith and kin, and once and again will have to fight for its booty before it gets it home; but do you think it tugs at the unwieldly carcase any the less for that? By and by, when the hard work is all over, and the splendid burden is at the nest door, success achieved, help be sure will be abundant. An officious crowd will laboriously assist in the easy task of rolling the half wasp down the hole, and the only one among them all that can remember the morning toil of pulling the dead thing out from among the roots, the sore struggle at noon with the scout from another nest, and the long afternoon when hope sickened almost to despair in the dusty ravines between the stones, is jostled from its hold (so grimly firm all day) of the goodly spoil. And the fussy mob of malingerers will take credit for the completion of the work! Beating up against the coming storm, who will help that crow? And when the sluice is opened who will lend a hand to the frog to help it stem the sudden rush of water? See how each bird keeps watch for itself. The bee-eater that grudges the air a single fly as it skims, wings level and tail fanwise, from perch to perch, has so quick an eye the while for the passing hawk that the ominous shadow has hardly formed upon the ground before the bird sees it, and with a quick note of terror is deep in the covert of the nearest tree. Meanwhile, the hoopoe, surely the daintiest of birds that walk the grass, has vanished from its place, the lyric bulbul has checked his song, the meditative crow pheasant—the Egbert among birds—is safe under a bush, and snug all of a row the Seven Sisters, their babble quenched for the moment, are perched high up in the bair. The hawk has passed, and on a sudden see, each in its place, all the little ministers of Nature!

Listen to that koel. Does its cry teach you nothing, in

its monotony? Men may come and men may go, but this year is the same as the last was and as the next will be. And every life in it is a crescendo of hopes, ending in a strangle, a straining after just that one note higher which the voice cannot reach without breaking.

What a height that bird is in the air! Vulture, or kite, or eagle, too far off to tell. Would it be a punishment if after death our deathless part went from the pedestrian life of man to the cloud-life of eagles? With wings that never tire, and no importunate appetites, to circle out a life in those "emptier wastes" of the Upper Chambers of the air than which, as one has finely remarked, no dungeon beneath a mountain can be more impenetrably secret. There, ranging with your peers alone, to overlook for a century the drama of the Earth! When Rome's empire was in flames at every corner, the eagles of the sky saw the eagles of the Legions swooping from sea to sea, the mightiest conflicts ever waged by a nation. Eagles must have seen Atlantis sink!

UNDER THE BANYAN.

"THE fig-tree, not that kind for fruit renown'd,
But such as at this day to Indians known
In Malabar and Deccan spreads her arms,
Branching so broad and long that in the ground
The bended twigs take root, and daughters grow
About the mother tree, a pillar'd shade,
High o'erarch'd and echoing walls between.
There oft the Indian herdsman, shunning heat,
Shelters in cool and tends his pasturing herds
At loop-holes cut through the thickest shade."

ILTON'S picture is delightful enough. The "Indian Herdsman," seated in cool-shaded ease, watches through a loop-hole in the dense foliage his grazing flocks. Unhappily it is not quite to the life. But another, hardly less quaint, is.

The sun is at its hottest, the languid flocks remember the pillared shade and, their morning hunger sated, turn, with only one mind to all their bodies, in the direction of their noon-day shelter. No need now for the herdsman to affect to lead his flock. It has already trotted ahead of him, and when, at the corner, the foremost has seen the welcome grove, the whole train breaks into a canter. A minute later and neither goat nor sheep is in sight. The herdsman follows at his leisure; all his scanty clothing swathed round his head, and in his hand a spray of unripe mango fruitlings, windfalls strangely overlooked by the cripple who watches the tree, and of which by specious tending of a wayward goat, the simple herdsman had possessed himself to season a mess withal. And still merry over the harmless felony, he passes singing (save the mark!) a ditty of the kind that pleases such. Let us follow him under the banyan. Does not the sight remind you of some Puritan desecration of a church?

Along the pillared aisles, so dim of light, so loftily o'er-arched, the bleating folk are scattered. Some, distracted among the many nooks that invite repose, wander about at a loss where to settle. "This way and that, dividing the swift mind, intent" to sleep. Others, the older heads, have clustered picturesquely, sheep and goats together, at the very threshold, making themselves comfortable at once. On every root a kid or lamb has perched itself, and the game they play is an old acquaintance, of very simple rules—"Tom Tiddler's ground." The herdsman meanwhile has found his own corner, has driven off the kid that affected to dispute possession, and (who so skilful as a native?) has blown three sticks into a blaze, and is cooking his meal. Beyond him, in another corner, a party of travellers have turned from the high road to bivouac. The red-curtained wagon stands by them tilted up; and tethered between two of the banyan's pillars the pony slouches to discuss his melancholy provender. A dog squats by—near enough to smell the food, too far off for any sudden lunge of staff. Beyond these again, we find, hanging head downwards in clusters and rows, the residents of the place, a colony of flying-foxes—an uncomely show and an unsavoury company. But in spite of "vampyres," herds, and travellers, there is yet space enough under the banyan for solitude. Thread your way through the cloistered labyrinth of stem and bough, and whichever way you turn you will chance upon a retreat that, if you are of my kind, will tempt you to loiter, and, loitering, will delight you. Here is one.

Fit haunt for fawn or buskined nymph, a bower for Osiris' self—call him Noah or Bacchus as you will—when the burden of the summer's sun has overtaken him in his cups; a divan clean-swept, and garnished with sylvan seats, for his company of Bassarids and Bacchanals. Have you soul enough to shut your eyes and think Pan come again with all his happy rout? Raise your altars to Aditi, the Infinite Expanse, mother of all things. Pile up on it the green stuff grateful to Prithivi, the Broad One, the Earth. Strew the ground with tender foliage, and here, though the days of the Floralia be just gone,—here in India, and arid May holding his breath from heat,—you may conjure up any of the woodland scenes of "Endymion," and people it with all the Dryad folk. To help your imagination a kid peeps in at you. Simulating surprise, it skips sideways on to the gnarled root. But you are dull company, it says, and another sidelong skip takes it to the ground again, and away along the green vista it frisks to find a playmate. Amalthea will be here anon to look for it. A flash of crimson and gold and burnished bronze, and, see, over against you has perched the prophetic bird, with strong bill divining the secrets of the central bole, fluttering the creviced things that in the heart of the wood tunnel their mole galleries, and dragging to day the mystery-loving worm. Hark! It was Picus calling. With a flash of crimson and gold and burnished bronze the augur's bird is gone. Surely the company will be here soon. But you will have warning of their coming, the fluty reed and the tinkling sheep-bell. Stay a while longer. Trail some bright flowered creeper, the gorgeous trumpet-flower and full-scented clematis, about and between the green pilasters that crowd you round, and give your fancy a long tether. A glimpse of garden luxury snatched from Daphne by Orontes! A nook on Cithæron's side, the haunt of Mænads! a bower in Cyprus for the dove-drawn goddess' self.

And this reminds me of a protest I have often wished to make against those dull folk who "teach the bidden blush to rise" when Aphrodite is invoked. I am no apostle of the Paphian, and I hate sparrows. But I would remind the "stupidly good" that when they bridle at the love-queen's name, it is only to flatter their own uncouth interpretation of the great goddess. They should remember that in the Greeks' mythology the lover of Adonis was also the sunlight of the grimy home of hard-handed Labour. That though she proved weak when severally sued by the Gods of Valour, of Eloquence and of Wisdom, she always went attended by the modest Graces. These stole from the wine her lovers drank with her all that suggests your sensitive shudder, and quickened and made bright by charms of mind and demeanour the tedious lives of men. Remember this. The Greek that would compass Aphrodite had first to woo Euphrosyne and her maiden sisters.

And therefore I said that the sun-proof bower here under the banyan was, if you would have it so, a bower fit even for "the sweet Cyprian's" self.

Let out your fancy like (some one has said it before me) a "cockchafer tied by the leg." Kick out in your little circle and sprawl over it. Range for fantasies in cramped Laputas. Call up some mimic steward of the Sacred Things, to tell us what we did not know before—"the chief things of the ancient mountains and the precious things of the everlasting hills." Sense or nonsense makes little difference lying here. Around you the air tinted with the deep-sea green, above you the restless waves of foliage. The floor beneath your feet is as clean swept as the sea-floor. The ruddy fallen figs replace the shells. Further on mayhap you will find old Nereus couched in sea-drift, or the noisy Triton, his "wreathed shell" beside him, and his cheeks, even in his dreams, puffed to call together the glancing nymphs.

Avoid only the Sahara of common speech. It has but one perennial spring in all its dreary circle, its source the bare rocks of scandal, and bitter its waters—Marah. Forget for the hour your past, horrid with splinters of hopes. Do not think of the future, smooth though it be with good intentions. And the present! It is yesterday, to-day, and to-morrow, three turns of the glass only—no more, though even you be a Macrobian. "The great sea is bound with a little sand!" And of parsley was made the crown of the victors in the Isthmian games! The harlequin empires glitter and go. Remember the Seven Sleepers. By reason of the wrath of Pagan Rome they fled to a cave "with the gadding vine o'ergrown," and slept. It was only for the space of three men's lives; yet lo! when they awaked it was to find the Golden House of the Cæsar, "*semper* Augustus," untenanted, and all Europe Christian!

Your work can spare your thoughts for an hour. Call up forest fantasies for your pleasure. Unnail your mind from the everlasting pump, and let it loose among Norwegian pines, among the beeches and the firs of the Hartz, the oaks and cheer of the Himalayan range. You will meet strange company. At the Feast of Firs the Bear Kings revelling in woody Astor; on Munga Parbat the dainty Peri or awful Harginn; in Thuringian woods the willow goblin; in the Black Forest the Erl König and his elfin court—all the sprites of story. Idle dreaming enough, but dreams are wholesome, let doctors twaddle as they will. They were given us to lessen the remorseless distance between earth and heaven, this world and the next, and, by familiarizing it, to make less dreadful to the living the life after death. It is in dreams that the German stories make the elves steal human souls; in dreams that the people of the Philippines make their old men pass into the forms of old trees. Among the people of the Chilian coast souls of men that have benefited their kind when living continue, as cocoa-nut palms, to benefit them after death. In Burmah at this day our Government pays to the headman of forest tracts a fee "murung" for appeasing the manes of their ancestors lodged in old sal-trees.

The trees have been called "God's crops;" but this, as compassing their whole dignity, is as inadequate as if they had been called "the aviaries of God." They are more than mere providers of food and exhausters of the soil. To them in no mean degree is entrusted the regulation of the temperature and the rain-fall; and among their great functions are the sanitation and the fertility of the earth. The trees are the Vicars of God. Nor are they altogether the ministers of Man. They at times defy him. At all times they are jealously on his track, relentless, taking advantage of his negligence and tiring labour. Before him man clears the forest: behind him the forest springs up again. And in the end the trees may conquer.

Under the Banyan.

Find if you can any of the great cities of Mexico or of Anam. Even his temporary triumphs man owes only to the want of union in the vegetable world. One-half the trees will not grow where the other half thrive. If every plant were universally indigenous, man could not keep his footing on the soil for a day !

Once in the world's story the trees, putting aside their rivalries, allied themselves together to thrust man, the destroyer, from the earth. They came up in all their strength. Leagues of tamarind shoulder to shoulder and in a great phalanx covering half an empire, the sun-proof mangoes; the peepuls, restless oceans of foliage, and the bamboos by forests so close stemmed that not a quail might slip by them. The banyans conjoined their pillared mazes, roofing in a continent, and with them paced in serried ranks the stout-limbed contingents of the sal and teak. From all the mountain slopes swept down in torrents the relentless pines, and, shuddering the hills as they came, the army of the hardy oaks. The soughing of the firs and deodars as they rushed aslope upon the devoted plains could be heard above the thunder of the rocks which, as they dragged out their roots, rolled in avalanches from the riven hills. And so, behind them desolation and an earth torn to its very bowels, the giants of the forest rolled up before their leafy surges the whole animal world, the shrubs and undergrowth sweeping clean in their track, and at last they drove Man into the sea ! And so, says the Vishnu Purana, the wind could not blow, and the sun was shut out, and for ten thousand centuries the earth was desolate of moving things. But at last the patient gods wearied of the intolerance of the presumptuous vegetables, and came down to the help of man, and smote the banded forests with swords of flame, till they had cleared a space where the sun could shine, the wind could blow, and man again possess the soil. And then it was (though the Purán does not say so) that the gods drove the trees asunder, a prototype of the confusion of Babel, giving to each a separate nature, so that they might never again unite to defy heaven—

> "To mock the majesty of man's high birth;
> Despise his bulwarks and unpeople earth."

About "Tree worship" I have read *me pœnitet* nothing, though many and very wise have been the writers. But I can understand for myself how every nation in its infancy, casting about for a fitting symbol of the Great Spirit, should have worshipped trees.

> "It seems idolatry with some excuse
> When our forefather Druids, in their oaks
> Imagined sanctity."

The Brahmans give to trees the perceptions of pleasure and pain. And with that bright people that saw Pan in all their pines, Dionysus in every vine, and Athene among their olives, who feels not a liberal sympathy? It is no fear of Silvanus' wrath, nor of all the ill the Dryads may work me that makes me confess an enthusiasm for the conceit

Under the Banyan.

that personified the trees, that enshrined religion and enthroned letters in green groves. The Achæan League is now only a name; the oaks and beeches of Dodona have fallen to the woodman's axe, and all fellow-citizens alike of the one Necropolis, are now the rivals of the Academe. And yet I revere that old greatness that chose for the conferences of its patriots, the dignity of its gods, and the wisdom of its men, the splendour of the shadow of trees.

And Cyrus, dying, gave orders that his body should be buried *Under the Trees.*

CPSIA information can be obtained
at www.ICGtesting.com
Printed in the USA
LVOW04s1142250216
476642LV00020B/396/P

9 781166 457723